THE ROAD TO STRATFORD

THE
ROAD TO STRATFORD

by

FRANK O'CONNOR *pseud*

O'Donovan

METHUEN & CO. LTD., LONDON
36 Essex Street, Strand, W.C. 2

First published in 1948

PR 2900
S520
co. 2

CATALOGUE NO. 3729/U

THIS BOOK IS PUBLISHED IN COMPLETE
CONFORMITY WITH THE AUTHORIZED
ECONOMY STANDARDS

PRINTED IN GREAT BRITAIN

For
OLIVER ROBERTSHAW

I

WE identify William Shakespeare first in the world of letters by a bad joke. Up to the age of thirty it would have needed a surgical operation to convince him that puns about 'deer' and 'hart' were not the best jokes and the most touching allusions in the world. The only part of the Shakespeare legend we can confidently pronounce true on the face of it is that which says he had to leave Stratford because of a misunderstanding with Sir Thomas Lucy— 'Lousy Lucy' as he called him—about poaching. For years his literary capital—apart from a large collection of proverbs which he trotted out on every possible occasion— was an obviously first-hand acquaintance with deer, dogs, horses and hawks, and when we read his early plays like 'Titus Andronicus' and 'Henry VI', certain words begin to stick in our minds as they stuck in his, words like 'paling' and 'park', 'hart', and 'single' and 'bay', and we begin to gather the impression of a most enjoyably mis-spent youth. Even without knowing that he had got a girl older than himself into trouble, we should have to agree that there was probably something to be said in favour of 'Lousy Lucy' who has had the misfortune to acquire the most ghastly sort of immortality, all because of John Shakespeare's wild son.

A wild boy he certainly was, in spite of the proverbs, who left home not altogether of his own free will and with a certain resentful air of braggadocio which comes out in his plays, even the earliest.

> Such wind as scatters young men through the world
> To seek their fortunes further than at home
> Where small experience grows.

'Home-keeping youth have ever homely wits,' he was to write later, without remembering the fable of the fox and the grapes, and even when he had returned in middle age, a wealthy, travelled man, he could still look out complacently at the home-keeping youths of his own generation and fancy them envying him and regretting their lost opportunities.

> What should we speak of
> When we are old as you? when we shall hear
> The rain and wind beat dark December, how
> In this our pinching cave shall we discourse
> The freezing hours away?

But home-keeping youth have the initial advantage of a settled home, and the adventurous Shakespeare drifted into acting which was no career for a fastidious young man. On the whole, it was a bad time for fastidious young men who hadn't an independent income. Most of the literary men of Shakespeare's day, though university-trained, were outcasts, almost outlaws, with the half-savage, unsocial mentality of their kind. An actor, more particularly an actor who had no share in the company, was far lower in the social scale even than they. The advantage of his London season was conditioned by the Plague which might banish him for years to the provinces. Even in London he played in inn-yards and makeshift theatres, in broad daylight and the open air, the companion of music-hall turns, clowns, tumblers and dancers. His theatre with its stage jutting out into the audience, was part of that betwixt-and-between state of things which we associate with Elizabethan England; its architecture which is half Renaissance, half Gothic, and its prose: something rather isolated by its geographical and religious position from the main current of art and thought. So too the plays in which he acted, written by university men who had come down in the world, were less according to 'the law of writ' than 'the liberty'; less in the manner of classical models than that of a wild, popular art in which only the ornaments came from classical tradition.

Even the style of performance must have been markedly different from ours, for the protruding stage makes it so difficult for us to imagine how it appeared to contemporaries that we find even a great scholar like Granville Barker writing of 'the semi-circle of the audience' as though the Elizabethan actor acted in one direction only. To Shakespeare the audience must have been a circle, and when Hamlet spoke 'To be or not to be' he cannot have stood facing one way but must have swept about the stage, hurling one phrase to the left, another to the right, like an orator at an open-air meeting. In the same way when Polonius and he were together on the stage they cannot have kept the alignment which modern actors keep but must have moved about one another like boxers and fencers, so that the audience saw them from every side.

We may, accordingly, if we choose, imagine our young scapegrace riding a cheap nag or stealing a lift on the baggage wagon as the weary procession of mummers passed through the hopfields in summer. Outside some little town they would form up their ragged finery, and with trumpets blowing and feathered hats tossing parade the town in the manner of a modern circus. In the inn-yard they would fall to the erection of their stage, and the afternoon would see the townspeople paying their pennies as they came in off the street, the more respectable paying an extra penny to mount into the sheltered gallery. A trumpeter would sound a blast, and the young man with the long sensitive face and intense eyes would appear and perform his part in one of those preposterous plays which in after life would make him shriek with laughter. The light would fade; the players

3

would perform their dance, and the audience go home, leaving him to the freedom of the public-houses. The platform and the finery would be packed up—

> And all our beauty and our trim decays
> Like courts removing or like ended plays.

Coming on towards morning he would wake and hear the trampling of horses and the voices of early stirring carters in the cobbled yard. 'I think this be the most villainous house in all London road for fleas' and even as he recorded the phrase with a smile of amusement his heart would turn over with self-pity.

> O do thou for my sake with Fortune chide,
> The guilty goddess of my harmful deeds
> Who did not better for my life provide
> Than public means that public manners breeds.

Bᴙ October, 1592, when we first hear of him in London, twenty-eight years old and with a couple of plays to his name, Shakespeare had already managed to attract some aristocratic friends, influential enough to make Thomas Nashe and Henry Chettle repudiate the authorship of certain slanders on himself and Marlowe contained in an alleged work by the poet, Robert Greene, recently dead.

'Yes, trust them not,' are the words ascribed to the dying Greene when speaking of actors, 'for there is an upstart Crow, beautified with our feathers, that with his *Tiger's heart wrapped in a Player's hide*, supposes he is as well able to bombast out a blank verse as the best of you: and being an absolute *Johannes factotum*, is in his own conceit the only Shakescene in a country.'[1] The first italicised passage is, of course, a parody of Shakespeares' 'O Tiger's heart wrapped in a woman's hide' from '3 Henry VI'.

Nashe instantly retorted to this in a new edition of his 'Piers Penniless'. 'Other news I am advertised of, that a scald, trivial, lying pamphlet called Greene's Groatsworth of Wit is given out to be of my doing. God never have care of my soul, but utterly renounce me if the least word or syllable in it proceeded from my pen, or if I were in any way privy to the writing or printing of it.'[2]

Then Chettle, a compositor and hack-writer, added to this in a book registered for publication on December 8th. 'About three months since died M. Robert Greene, leaving many papers in sundry booksellers' hands, among other his Groatsworth of Wit, in which a letter written to divers playmakers is offensively by one or two of them taken; and

---

[1] *Greene's Groatsworth of Wit* (Bodley Head Quartos).
[2] *Piers Penniless' Supplication to the Devil* (Bodley Head Quartos).

because on the dead they cannot be avenged, they wilfully forge in their conceits a living author: and after tossing it to and fro, no remedy but it must light on me. How I have all the time of my conversing in printing hindered the bitter inveighing against scholars, it hath been very well known; and how in that I dealt, I can sufficiently prove. With neither of them that take offence was I acquainted, and with one of them I care not if I never be: the other, whom at that time I did not so much spare as since I wish I had, for that as I have moderated the heat of living writers, and might have used my own discretion (especially in such a case) the author being dead, that I did not, I am as sorry as if the original fault had been my fault, because myself have seen his demeanour no less civil than he excellent in the quality he professes: besides, divers of worship have reported his uprightness of dealing which argues his honesty, and his facetious grace in writing, that approves his art. For the first, whose learning I reverence, and at the perusing of Greene's book, struck out what then in conscience I thought he in some displeasure writ; or had it been true, yet to publish it was intolerable; him I would wish to use me no worse than I deserve. I had only in the copy this share; it was ill-written, as sometimes Greene's hand was none of the best, licensed it must be ere it could be printed, which could never be if it might not be read. To be brief I writ it over, and as near as I could followed the copy, only in that letter I put something out, but in the whole book not a word in, for I protest it was all Greene's, not mine, nor Master Nashe's, as some un-justly have affirmed. Neither was he the writer of an Epistle to the second part of *Gerileon*, though by the workman's error, T.N. were set to the end; that I confess to be mine, and repent it not.'[1]

I have quoted these over-familiar passages in full because

[1] *Kindheart's Dream* (Bodley Head Quartos).

in spite of their familiarity they seem to me generally mis-read. To begin with, considering that Shakespeare and Marlowe were apparently both satisfied that Greene had nothing to do with 'Greene's Groatsworth of Wit' it is hard luck on Greene's memory that almost every writer on Shakespeare should treat it as his. What I take from the documents is that, for some reason which is not apparent to us, 'Greene's Groatsworth of Wit' was immediately recognised as a forgery and attributed to Nashe, who, whether or not he had anything to do with it, took fright; and that Shakespeare, accompanied by 'divers of worship', called on the printer and discovered that the manuscript had not been in the handwriting of Greene but in that of the compositor, Chettle. It would seem that Chettle was interviewed by Shakespeare and his aristocratic friends or else sought an interview with them in the theatre (he admits to having seen Shakespeare act); that Shakespeare was 'civil' and that Chettle explained how he came to make a fair copy of Greene's manuscript before submitting it to the licensing authorities. As the proof of this was in his own possession, and the revered Master Nashe had pro-claimed the screed a forgery, we must presume that he also told them he had destroyed the original. Asked how it came about that a certain publication called 'Gerileon' contained an item signed 'T.N.' which was not the work of Master Nashe, he admitted his authorship and blamed the mistake on the compositor. Chettle was an obliging poor devil. When Harvey later took Nashe to task for the words he had written of 'Greene's Groatsworth of Wit', Chettle furnished Nashe with an extraordinary testimonial which begins: 'I hold it no good manners, Mr. Nash, being but an artificer, to give Dr. Harvey the lie, though he have deserved it by publishing in print you have done me wrong, which privately I never found. . . .'[1] In such a fix and in such an

1 Nashe, *Works*, ed. McKerrow.

obvious fright he could hardly do less for Shakespeare, so while repeating his insults to Marlowe (then very much under a cloud) he composed an abject apology to Shakespeare and a complete withdrawal to Nashe.

To put it mildly, one cannot believe daylight from Chettle. I can only conclude that he was a party to the forgery of 'Greene's Groatsworth of Wit' though I find it hard to believe that he was talented enough to be the author; and that the 'divers of worship' who were so indifferent to what was said of Marlowe were friendly both with Shakespeare and Nashe. Harvey's reference to Nashe as 'a young Babington' suggests that one at least of his patrons was a Catholic, and Nashe's dedication of an obscene poem to 'Lord S.' that this was Lord Strange, for whose company Shakespeare almost certainly wrote some of his early plays. If Strange is the lord with the company of players who had earlier patronised Marlowe and Kyd, we know from a pathetic letter of Kyd to Puckering that by 1592 he was aware of Marlowe's atheism and had withdrawn his protection. Furthermore, as within the following months Shakespeare dedicated 'Venus and Adonis' and Nashe 'Jack Wilton' to the Earl of Southampton we have substantial grounds for believing that he was another of the 'divers of worship'. Nashe's patron, Sir George Carey, whose father, Lord Hunsdon, later took over Strange's company with Shakespeare as a shareholder, was probably a third.

When in 1594 George Chapman dedicated 'The Shadow of Night' to Matthew Royden, it was certainly for want of a better mark among this group: 'most ingenious Derby (i.e. Strange) deep-searching Northumberland, and skill-embracing heir of Hunsdon' (Carey); and as certainly this had been brought about through the ill-offices of some literary man associated with them. 'How then,' Chapman exclaims bitterly, 'may a man stay his marvelling to see passion-driven men, reading but to curtail a tedious hour, and altogether hide-bound with affection to great men's fancies, take upon them as killing censures as if they were judgment's butchers, or as if the life of truth lay tottering in their verdicts. Now what a *supererogation* in wit is this, to think skill so mightily *pierced* with their loves . . . etc.'[1] As the reference to 'Piers' Supererogation' suggests, the butcher was probably Nashe, though the Rival Poet sonnets may well refer to the same occasion, and I have little doubt that the 'Muses that Fame's loose feathers beautify and such as scorn to tread the theatre' of the Chapman sonnets published in 1595, were Shakespeare's.

Shakespeare's earliest work consists of a bloodthirsty tragedy, 'Titus Andronicus', a brilliant comedy, 'The Taming of the Shrew' and a group of four historical plays dealing with Henry VI and Richard III. 'Titus Andronicus' is usually regarded as not being Shakespeare's at all. I am afraid I think it is entirely his. 'The Taming of the Shrew' is also believed to be only partly his, and most editors limit him to the Induction and the Petruchio-Catharine episodes. Thus, according to Fleay and Chambers, in iii. 2 lines 129 to 250 are by the second author. When two great scholars select from a scene of over 250 lines twenty-one as being by somebody other than Shakespeare, there should, I feel, be something spectacularly unShakespearean about them. On the contrary, they appear to me to be typically Shakespearean. Two of the twenty-one run:

Which once performed, let all the world say no,
I'll keep my own despite of all the world[2]

Shakespeare was particularly attached to that particular phrase and even cadence. 'Though I once gone to all the

---

[1] Chapman, *Shadow of Night*.   [2] *T.S.*, III. 2.

world must die';[1] 'You are my All the World';[2] 'That All the World besides methinks are dead.[3] Richard III is ready 'to undertake the death of all the world',[4] while Constance says 'My life, my joy, my food, my All the World.'[5] In 'Titus Andronicus' we get:

> I care not, I, knew she and all the world;
> I love Lavinia more than All the world.[6]

It occurs again in 'A Midsummer Night's Dream':

> For you in my respect are All the world,
> Then how can it be said I am alone
> When all the world is here to look on me?[7]

The phrase occurs in two other places in the play (ii. 1. 284 and iv. 2. 35) and the same authorities assign *one* to the collaborator. Bless our poor criticism from underminers and blowers-up! There was no collaborator.

The most interesting of the group to the critic are the historical plays, for here, in some sort of sequence, we can see how Shakespeare picked up the poet's job. The first part of 'Henry VI' is a wretched production; that goes without saying, though I am far from convinced either that it is a Shakespearean revision of a play by a syndicate of authors or one written as a member of such a syndicate. I have no idea how this dim, crude, least Shakespearean of plays seems to be the new play of Henry VI which Henslowe records as first produced in the spring of 1592 at a time when we know from 'Greene's Groatsworth of Wit' that the fine third part must already have been in existence; but I do not for a moment believe in the 'hands' which scholars identify with such care, and even Sir E. K.

---

[1] *Sonnets*, 81.   [2] *Sonnets*, 112.   [3] *Sonnets*, 112.   [4] *Richard III*, I. 2.
[5] *King John*, III. 4.   [6] *Titus*, II. 1.   [7] *M.N.D.*, II. 2.

Chambers fails to persuade me that 'Had Death been French then Death had died today'[1] or 'No more can I be severed from your side than can yourself yourself in twain divide'[2] were not written by Shakespeare.

The second part is better only in the sense that it is more competent, and here there is no question of Shakespeare's hand for in the Jack Cade scenes we can all recognise his characteristic obsession with the idea of public order. This was a theme which haunted him to the day of his death. He had a real obsession with mobs, as if at some time he had become caught up in one and found himself unable to escape. He draws them with great vividness and even humour as in the lines he gives the old lady in 'Sir Thomas More' who wanted to hear More speak because he had made 'my brother, Arthur Watchins, Sergeant Safe's yeoman' but he always reveals his fear. Nothing in 'Julius Caesar' is so vivid as the scene in which the mob tears the poet, Cinna, asunder. By the time he wrote 'Troilus and Cressida' and particularly 'Hamlet' his fear had become hysterical, and in all the later plays tragedy is emphasised by the insistence on the disappearance of class distinctions: 'preordinance and first decree', 'the primogenitive and due of birth' are falling into contempt; the peasant is galling the courtier's kibe; reverence 'that angel of the world' which 'makes distinction between high and low' is in bad shape; 'the odds is gone', 'all mannerly distinguishment left out between the prince and beggar' and the end of the world is obviously round the next corner.

But for all its weaknesses '2 Henry VI' steadily mounts and one can almost perceive the moment when Shakespeare felt Eleanor and Gloucester come alive under his hands. In later years he toyed with the idea of revising it, and even scribbled in a few lines on the margin in his mature style, the style of 'Macbeth'.

[1] *1 Henry VI*, IV. 6.   [2] *1 Henry VI*, IV. 5.

Be that thou hop'st to be or what thou art
Resign to death.[1]

For the rest the play has all the characteristics of the early Shakespeare: the weakness for proverbs; the fondness for sporting allusions; and a certain ponderous, coarse poetic power which you can feel even in a half dozen lines.

The gaudy, blabbing and remorseful day
Is crept into the bosom of the sea;
And now loud-howling wolves arouse the jades
That drag the tragic, melancholy night;
Who with their drowsy, slow and flagging wings
Clip dead men's graves, and from their misty jaws
Breathe foul, contagious darkness in the air.[2]

Knowing what we do, that is not what we should nowadays call a typical Shakespearean passage as we call the preceding line and a half Shakespearean; but it is typical of the earlier Shakespeare in what critics call his 'Marlovian' period. I don't think it owes anything to Marlow whose influence comes much later in his work. Marlowe was the one and only Playboy of the Western World, and I sometimes fancy John Synge must have had something more than an unconscious recollection of him when he christened his hero Christopher Mahon. When Marlowe went the round of the London pubs, roaring out his really atrocious blasphemies and defending unnatural vice and smoking (this before King James made smoking unfashionable) he was not so much expressing views which had been arrived at by any known process of reasoning as giving a lep to the east while bringing down the loy on the ridge of his da's skull and leaving him split to the breeches belt. His uproarious poetry talk, like Christy Mahon's, is full of

[1] *2 Henry VI*, III. I.   [2] *2 Henry VI*, IV. I.

radiance; Shakespeare's, as you can see even from those few lines which I have quoted, has no radiance at all. On the contrary, it is leaden and sinister. What Shakespeare has and Marlowe has not is weight. He is all the time trying to make his lines carry more and more weight. Sometimes he breaks their back with the burdens he heaps on them. Even in those few lines I have quoted there are no less than a dozen adjectives; you can see him at his favourite trick of loading up a noun with a whole string of adjectives as in 'The gaudy, blabbing and remorseful day' or 'Who with their drowsy, slow and flagging wings', and if I had continued to quote I should have had to produce others like 'And lofty, proud, encroaching tyranny' and 'Upon these paltry, servile, abject drudges'. As you can see, he doesn't worry very much about the meaning of the adjectives; he is satisfied if only there are plenty of them.

You can also see him building compounds under the impression that a compound is twice as effective as a simple word, as in the 'loud-howling' wolves, and a glance through this group of plays will reveal dozens of them: 'gentle-sleeping', 'earnest-gaping', 'bitter-searching', 'great-commanding' and even 'dead-killing' which some ingenious person might like to use as evidence of an Irish ancestry. In 'Romeo and Juliet', in the firm conviction that five words say five times as much as one, he writes: 'Beguiled, divorced, wronged, spited, slain.' And sometimes, by sheer mass, he does achieve an effect of extraordinary solemnity. 'The gaudy, blabbing and remorseful day' is a fine line, whatever it means, and Queen Margaret's 'I stood upon the hatches in the storm' is a magnificent line.

The opening scenes of '3 Henry VI' show Shakespeare in perfect command of this sort of poetry. They contain far finer lines than anything in the previous two parts, but they are the same sort of lines, and the effect they aim at is largely physical.

That raught (reached) at mountains with outstretched arms
Yet parted but the shadow with his hands[1]

These eyes that now are dimmed with death's black veil
Have been as piercing as the midday sun
To search the secret treasons of the world.[2]

'Richard III' is the masterpiece of this period, and a masterpiece it is, for all its violence, coarseness and vulgarity. Again, it is the same sort of poetry. 'I stood upon the hatches in the storm' or 'The gaudy, blabbing and remorseful day' are lines which might have come from the scene of Clarence's dream with its 'To gaze upon the secrets of the deep' or 'To find the empty, vast and wandering air';[3] and that particular kind of poetry went on in Shakespeare for some considerable time, because even in 'Edward III', 'King John', and 'The Comedy of Errors' we get lines like 'Even in the barren, bleak and fruitless air,'[4] or 'Of the old, feeble and day-weary sun';[5] 'And eyeless terror of all-ending night';[6] 'Before the always-wind-obeying deep'[7] and 'Lord of the wide world and wild watery seas'.[8]

It is, I think, great poetry. It is certainly poetry which aims at a knock-out; which tries to make your hair stand on end. The trouble about it is that it is only poetry. Shakespeare, like Marlowe, was at this time mainly a poet, and to every true poet poetry is an end in itself. The medium is more important than what is said through it, or if you care to put it in another way, to the poet plays are merely an excuse to write fine verse, and the stronger the situations, the better it is likely to be for the verse. Thus every poet in the theatre has a natural tendency to melodrama which

[1] *3 Henry VI*, I. 4.   [2] *3 Henry VI*, v. 4.   [3] *Richard III*, I. 4.
[4] *Edward III*, I. 2.   [5] *King John*, v. 4.   [6] *Edward III*, IV. 4.
[7] *C. of E.*, I. I.   [8] *C. of E.*, II. I.

14

he is bound to try and control. It was not only the unsophisticated Tudor audiences who liked tubs of blood. The poets got quite a kick from them too.

But drama is of a younger house. Poetry is about yourself and other people in relation to yourself; drama is about other people and only about yourself in relation to other people; and it is only occasionally that the subject which makes for poetry also makes for drama. Marlowe's plays tell us a great deal more about Marlowe than they do about their heroes; so do Yeats', and so do the Henry VI plays of Shakespeare. In life he must have been an energetic, ambitious, passionate man, for all the people in these plays are cut out of that particular bit of cloth; but the spectacle of so many people being energetic, ambitious and passionate together creates an extraordinarily sombre effect, an overpowering effect, as though we were being smothered in an atmosphere of subjectivity; and we find ourselves longing to get out again into the air and light. Have you noticed how all the fine lines in these plays are sombre? How there seems to be none that has lightness or grace, and how they seem to attract gloomy imagery like mountains and seas, darkness and storm?

Drama happens only when the poet's hard shell of subjectivity cracks, and when he is half-in, half-out of his shell, like the girl in Hardy's poem of the Desecrated Churchyard who feared 'lest half of her should rise herself and half some sturdy strumpet'. What remains of the poet when he has expressed the objective reality of his characters is a sort of lyrical quintessence which he uses only in the last resort, when his imagination refuses to follow them further or when finally he chooses to identify himself with them in the last gesture of all.

When Shakespeare had completed this group of plays he had reached a dead end, had 'reached at mountains with outstretched arms and parted but the shadow with his hands'. But during those years something happened to crack the shell, for even in '3 Henry VI' he was feeling his way towards another sort of excellence, the excellence of 'Richard II' and 'Edward III' which has nothing shadowy about it. Out of the roar of the Henry plays comes just one speech which shows us what the next phase in Shakespeare's development was to be: the speech of the pious King, cobweb-thin but piercingly true.

What time the shepherd blowing of his nails . . .

And:

His cold, thin drink out of his leathern bottle.[1]

'And after the thunder a still, small voice. And it was so.'

---

[1] *3 Henry VI*, II. 5.

III

WE are sometimes inclined to ignore one important
fact about Shakespeare's life: that, like many other
provincials, he developed exceedingly late. He was close on
thirty when 'Richard III' was produced. Within five years
he was the greatest of European writers; within ten perhaps
the greatest writer who has ever lived. Throughout the
plays after 'Richard III' we see a development which one
would only suppose possible in an adolescent, and parallel
with this, we have the sonnets which accompany the development and seem to describe a personal emotional
disturbance sufficient to account for it. This alone would
be enough to justify any curiosity we might feel about them.

The story, so far as we can gather it, is that Shakespeare
became deeply attached to a good-looking young aristocrat.
At the same time he was in love with a black-haired married
woman 'of noted misbehaviour with old and young' if we
are to believe himself. The woman was attracted by
Shakespeare's friend who made her his mistress, leaving
the poet doubly bereaved. Unfortunately, if the sonnets tell
us this, which is far from certain, they tell us very little else.
They do not tell us who the young man was, and all the
identifications of him are mere guesswork; they do not tell
us when the episode occurred or where. They were written
from time to time, sometimes two, sometimes four to a
sheet, and by the time they reached the printer the sheets
had been shuffled and the continuity destroyed.

They are extraordinary poems by a most extraordinary
man. The sonnets to the woman begin with jocose compli-
ments and degenerate into something very like scurrility.
The sonnets to the friend begin in adoration, but this is
soon almost smothered in reproaches and complaints. They

oscillate in the most disturbing way between a sociable jocosity and a shuddering sensibility; a sonnet will begin in the urbane convention of *amour courtois* with a line like 'These pretty wrongs that liberty commits' and suddenly burst into 'Ay, me, but yet thou might'st my seat forbear'[1] which immediately tears the whole delicate web of convention to shreds, and makes what has preceded it sound vulgar and stupid.

One word in particular is repeated over and over again until it dins itself into the reader's brain.

Take all my loves, my love, yea, take them all . . .[2]

Take all my comfort of they worth and truth . . .[3]

And by a part of all thy glory live . . .[4]

For whether beauty, worth or wealth or wit,
Or any of these all, or all, or more . . .[5]

All frailties that besiege all kinds of blood . . .
To leave for nothing all thy sum of good,
For nothing this wide universe I call
Save thou, my Rose, in it thou art my all.[6]

Or gluttoning on all, or all away . . .[7]

Sin of self love possesseth all mine eye,
And all my soul, and all my every part . . .[8]

Thy bosom is endeared with all hearts . . .
And there reigns Love and all love's loving parts,
And all those friends that I thought buried . . .
And thou, all they, hast all the all of me.[9]

[1] *Sonnets*, 41. [2] *Sonnets*, 40. [3] *Sonnets*, 37. [4] *Sonnets*, 37. [5] *Sonnets*, 37.
[6] *Sonnets*, 109. [7] *Sonnets*, 75. [8] *Sonnets*, 62. [9] *Sonnets*, 31.

To me at least, this suggests a lacerated sensibility, a man of great sincerity but of the wildest extremes of emotion, completely powerless against his own attachments; and the very devil for the bright young things of the sixteenth century who must so often have bidden him 'take life easy as the grass grows on the weirs'.

Apart from certain minor readjustments suggested by the Arden editor and Sir Edmund Chambers, no attempt at rearranging the sonnets has ever proved convincing. A simple test is the sequence of ten sonnets on Immortality in each of which the concluding couplet consoles the friend for the ravages of time by promising him an immortality of print. These at least, one feels, should go together, but Professor Tucker Brooke and Sir Denys Bray agree on dispersing them further. Professor Brooke makes the additional and very common mistake of treating the first seventeen sonnets as the beginning of the series, which on every ground of technique is impossible. The earliest may be a couple of short sequences; one on a journey, the other —a particularly silly one—about Eye and Heart at war for the privilege of contemplating the Friend's beauty. It contains one of the very few suppressions of the article in the sonnets; a form of clumsiness which Shakespeare quickly outgrew. This bit of nonsense, apparently modelled on Constable, probably dates from the publication of his sonnets in 1592. By 1592, Shakespeare, we know from Chettle's reference to 'divers of worship', had some powerful friends. The Friend and he had met in the spring: this was probably the spring of 1592, for the more commonly accepted date of 1593 is far too late.

The long sequence apologising for his silence and referring to a rival poet is considerably maturer in style but still far from faultless. In 'Greene's Groatsworth of Wit', the pamphlet containing the reference to Shakespeare as 'an upstart crow', there is an image of 'a player that being out of his part at his first entrance is fain to have the book to speak what he should perform';[1] and in Gabriel Harvey's description of the grief of Greene's mistress he describes Greene as one 'that a tenth muse honoured more being dead than all nine honoured him alive'.[2] It is hard to read these without thinking of Shakespeare's 'unperfect actor on the stage who with his fear is put beside his part'[3] and his 'tenth muse, ten times more in worth than those old nine which rhymers invocate';[4] and the fact that both occur in the Apologetic Muse sequence may possibly indicate that it was written shortly after September, 1592. The sonnets to the Dark Lady cannot, I feel, be much later. In Daniel's poem 'The Complaint of Rosamund', published in 1592, there is a line 'By the revenues of a wanton bed'[5] which seems to be echoed in Shakespeare's charge that the Dark Lady 'robbed other beds' revenues of their rents'.[6] I doubt if these and the Canker in the Rose sequence which preceded them can be dated later than 1593.

This date is also suggested by the two long poems, 'Venus and Adonis' (1593) and 'The Rape of Lucrece' (1594). They are of fundamental importance in the study of Shakespeare's development, because, like the frosty but beautiful Marriage sonnets, they are written with a wealth of craftsmanship which Shakespeare rarely expended on everyday tasks. They are generally treated as academic exercises. For instance, according to Dr. Harrison, Shakespeare, inspired by Marlowe's 'Hero and Leander', wrote 'Venus and Adonis', which might be politely described as a poem about a young man who didn't want to get married, printed it, and then set out to find a patron. He found one in the Earl of Southampton (also a young man who didn't want to get married) who introduced him to his household,

---

[1] *Greene's Groatsworth of Wit* (Bodley Head Quartos).
[2] Gabriel Harvey, *Four Letters* (Bodley Head Quartos).   [3] *Sonnets* 23.
[4] *Sonnets*, 33.   [5] Daniel, *Complaint of Rosamund*.   [6] *Sonnets*, 142.

where Shakespeare, following the fashion, wrote the sonnets advising him to get married.

I do not think that Shakespeare was influenced by 'Hero and Leander', nor am I altogether satisfied that Southampton is the person addressed in the sonnets; but anyhow, the trouble with this explanation is the obvious coincidence it involves, and Professor Wilson, with characteristic subtlety, side-steps it by suggesting that Shakespeare arrived on Southampton's doorstep one morning with a copy of 'Venus and Adonis' *and* the first seventeen sonnets, in which a nobleman whom Shakespeare had never met is addressed as his 'dear love' and advised to marry the girl his family has chosen for him.

There is stranger to follow, for Shakespeare and the Earl, according to the same eminent authorities, became fast friends, and Shakespeare entertained the Earl with another long poem, in which a poor man, Collatine, tells a princely friend, Tarquin, of the charms of his wife, Lucrece, and Tarquin, inflamed by the description, goes off and rapes her. Now Shakespeare, a poor man, was at this time the lover of the Dark Lady, and his aristocratic friend came on the scene and made her his mistress. Shakespeare had such uncanny luck with his long poems that it is small wonder he gave up writing them.

What I suggest, of course, is that if the poems are academic exercises, they are uncommonly prophetic; if not prophetic, they must be an artistic treatment of the situations described in the sonnets. As I feel sure that this is what they are, I find it hard to believe that Lord Southampton, to whom both are dedicated, can be the young man of the Dark Lady sonnets.

There is what seems to me a personal note about one particular passage in 'The Rape of Lucrece'. It refers to Tarquin.

> Those that much covet are with gain so fond
> For what they have not, that which they possess
> They scatter and unloose it. . . .[1]

This is repeated a little later when Shakespeare tells us how this 'ambitious foul infirmity'—

> In having much torments us with defect
> Of that we have; so then we do neglect
> The thing we have. . . .[2]

That 'the thing we have' was himself, slighted by a youthful Tarquin to whom he was deeply attached, is at least suggested by the re-emergence of the theme in almost identical words over a period of twenty years. It first comes back in 'Much Ado About Nothing' (1598) with a new concluding phrase which gives it its characteristic form— 'Ne'er loved till lost.'

> That which we have, we prize not to the worth
> Whiles we enjoy it, but being lacked and lost,
> Why then we rack the value. . . .[3]

We get it again in 'Measure for Measure' (1605): 'For what thou hast not, still thou striv'st to get, and what thou hast forget'st';[4] *three* times in 'All's Well That Ends Well' of the same date, with its 'You are loved, sir. They that least lend it you shall lack you first';[5] 'She whom I . . . since I have lost have loved';[6] and:

> Love that comes too late
> Like a remorseful pardon slowly carried
> To the great sender turns a sour offence,
> Crying 'That good that's gone.'[7]

---

[1] *R. of L.*   [2] *R. of L.*   [3] *M.A.N.*, IV. I.   [4] *M. for M.*, III. I.
[5] *A.W.E.W.*, I. 2.   [6] *A.W.E.W.*, V. 3.   [7] *A.W.E.W.*, V. 3.

We find it in 'Antony and Cleopatra' of 1607–8—'the ebbed man, ne'er loved till nothing worth comes deared by being lacked';[1] in 'Coriolanus' (1609)—'I shall be loved when I am lacked'[2] and it makes its final appearance in what was probably Shakespeare's last play, 'The Two Noble Kinsmen' (1613).

> For what we lack
> We laugh, for what we have are sorry, still
> Are children in some kind.[3]

Once more, the date I suggest for these sonnets seems to be corroborated by 'Willoughby's Avisa', a skit on 'The Rape of Lucrece' published in the same year as that poem, 1594. In this Henry Willoughby, a young aristocratic poet of West Knoyle in Wiltshire (a real person as Professor Hotson has shown, and a relative by marriage of Shakespeare's friend, Thomas Russell),[4] is described in a vain courtship of Avisa, wife of the owner of an inn called 'The George' or 'The George and Dragon' which Dr. Harrison in his brilliant edition of the poem identifies with the George at Sherborne in Dorset (not very far from West Knoyle and then the home of Sir Walter Ralegh).[5] He is encouraged by his friend 'W.S.', 'an old player', 'who not long before had tried the courtesy of the like passion, and was now newly recovered of the like infection'. It is significant that in 'King John', written probably in the same year, Shakespeare speaks of—

Saint George who swinged the Dragon and e'er since
Sits on his horse back at mine hostess' door.[6]

[1] *A.C.*, I. 4.   [2] *Cor.*, IV. I.   [3] *T.N.K.*, V. 4.
[4] Hotson, *I William Shakespeare* . . .
[5] Harrison, *Willoughby's Avisa* (Bodley Head Quartos).
[6] *King John* II. I.

23

The slight circumstantial evidence which might link 'Willoughby's Avisa' with the sonnets is that the Friend's name seems to have been 'Will', which might equally stand for 'Willoughby', and that there are a couple of sonnets, not in Shakespeare's manner, which refer to Bath, which is near West Knoyle. That the friend of the sonnets got the girl while Henry Willoughby did not would, of course, mean nothing; the skit would otherwise missfire. What is important is Sir Edmund Chambers' warning that 'the like passion' does not necessarily mean a passion for Avisa; it might equally mean a disappointment with another woman; the Dark Lady in fact.

To my mind, the most important evidence of all is that of 'Edward III', a play supposed by Tucker Brooke to be by Peele, by Robertson to be Greene's; by some Shakespearean scholars to contain two acts of Shakespeare. I have no doubt whatever that the play is entirely Shakespeare's. What appears to have happened is that when Shakespeare had written 'Richard III' he had come to the end of the York and Lancaster series so far as they could be dramatically presented, and immediately switched back and began again at the other end with 'Edward III' and 'Richard II' in that order. The play was registered for publication late in 1595 and published early in the following year, and as it is a regular playhouse text of a play which had had its run, it was presumably produced not later than the end of 1593 or the spring of 1594—that is to say at the time when Shakespeare was putting the finishing touches to 'The Rape of Lucrece'. It deals with a similar subject to the poem and in a similar way. King Edward makes love to the Countess of Salisbury who, as the dramatist is careful to remind us, defends herself more effectually than Lucrece 'whose ransacked treasury hath tasked the vain endeavours of so many pens'. In poem and play (as well as in the Dark Lady sonnets) the offence lies mainly in the offender's rank.

Lucrece says:

> The mightier man, the mightier is the thing
> That makes him honoured or begets him hate.[1]

Warwick in 'Edward III' says:

> The greater man, the greater is the thing
> Be't good or bad that he shall undertake.[2]

Shakespeare in the sonnets says:

> Lilies that fester smell far worse than weeds.[3]

Warwick in the play says:

> Lilies that fester smell far worse than weeds.[4]

It is even more curious in a play written at the time of the sonnets to find King Edward ordering his secretary Lodowick to write sonnets on his behalf to the Countess, and rejecting the first sonnet on the ground that it is inadequate. This is not only first-rate comedy; it is startlingly personal, and adds another question-mark to the sonnets themselves.

These are echoed everywhere through the play. In the beautiful love-scenes, Edward, interrupted in his love-making by the appearance of the Black Prince, murmurs as though he were remembering 'Thou art thy mother's glass and she in thee calls back the lovely April of her prime'[5] or Lucretius' 'Poor broken glass, I often did behold in thy sweet semblance my old age newborn':[6]

---

[1] *R. of L.*   [2] *Edward III*, II. I.   [3] *Sonnets*, 94.
[4] *Edward III*, II. I.   [5] *Sonnets*, 3.   [6] *R. of L.*

> I see the boy; oh, how his mother's face
> Modelled in his, corrects my strayed desire.[1]

There is the echo of another sonnet in the magnificent lines on Death.

> When to the great Star Chamber o'er our heads
> The universal sessions calls to count. . . .[2]

as well as frequent reminiscences like the man going forth without his cloak (paralleled in 'Richard III' by 'when clouds appear wise men put on their cloaks'); 'the adverse part' ('the adverse party' of 'Richard III' and the sonnets) and the 'scarlet ornaments'. Perhaps the most startling is the cry of delight with which the Countess of Salisbury welcomes her brother, with its echo of the loveliest of sonnets—'O summer's day!'[3] a mere catch in the breath like Laertes' 'O Rose of May!' or Charmian's 'O Eastern Star!' and the really remarkable fact that one line in 'Edward III' is the very proverb which forms the theme of the Dark Lady sonnets—'Too bright a morning breeds a louring day.'[4]

But the evidence which from my point of view clinches the question is the identity of style and subject matter with other Shakespearean plays of the same period; an identity which is beyond any possibility of imitation, even if the author of 'Edward III' needed to imitate anybody. Whatever the nature of Shakespeare's emotional experience, it had an immediate and pronounced effect on his work, which became more cautious, more restrained, more intellectual. This is particularly marked in the use of what I may call the 'reflexive' conceit in 'Richard III' and the long poems. 'Thyself thyself misuseth'[5] says Queen Elizabeth to Richard.

---

[1] *Edward III*, II. 2.　　[2] *Edward III*, II. 2.
[3] *Edward III*, I. 2.　　[4] *Edward III*, IV. 9.　　[5] *Richard III*, IV. 4.

'Myself myself confound'[1] retorts Richard. Of course, there is nothing unusual about the conceit itself, which is merely an elaborate way of saying 'You abuse yourself' or 'May I destroy myself'. But there is always an implication of antithesis. Everything contains its own opposite by which it is saved or destroyed; and it harmonises with a certain duality in the Elizabethan temperament which enabled it to act and at the same time to admire itself acting; or to see in art and literature patterns by which to measure its own behaviour, like Lucrece seeing in the picture of the Fall of Troy herself as Hecuba and Tarquin as Sinon. 'Shall I forget myself to be myself?' asks Queen Elizabeth again.[2] Probably the most characteristic convention of Elizabethan literature is the pattern.

> Do it by me, by me the lost Aspasia,
> And you shall find all true but the wild island.[3]

Nor is there anything peculiar to Shakespeare in the conceit. Daniel has phrases like 'thyself thyself deniest' and 'greatness greatness mars'. At the same time Shakespeare attached extraordinary importance to it for which I can find no parallel among contemporary writers. Adonis, by refusing to become the lover of Venus, becomes like the hero of the Marriage sonnets 'the tomb of his self-love to stop posterity':[4] 'So in thyself thyself art made away';[5] 'Narcissus so himself himself forsook.'[6] There is no hope for Tarquin 'When he himself himself confounds, betrays',[7] and he must 'himself himself seek every hour to kill'.[8] His crime has made Lucrece 'herself herself detest'.[9] Turning to 'Edward III', we find that the Black Prince must 'himself himself redeem'[10] and the Countess of Salisbury is not really

[1] *Richard III*, IV. 4.   [2] *Richard III*, IV. 4.
[3] Beaumont and Fletcher, *The Maid's Tragedy*, II. 2.
[4] *Sonnets*, 3.   [5] *V. & A.*   [6] *V. & A.*   [7] *R. of L.*   [8] *R. of L.*
[9] *R. of L.*   [10] *Edward III*, III. 5.

beautiful 'if that herself were by to stain herself'[1] ('Herself poised with herself in either eye' as in 'Romeo and Juliet'.)

The treatment of the conceit in 'Edward III' is quite remarkable. Warwick says 'Well may I tempt myself to wrong myself';[2] the Countess asks the King to 'Entreat thyself to stay awhile with me'[3] and he tells her to 'take thyself aside a little way and tell thyself a king doth dote on thee'.[4] Here the antithesis is complete; the character completely broken down and the two parts are conceived as addressing one another. By itself, of course, it is not an infallible sign of Shakespearean authorship, but when in a scene in '1 Henry VI' which Sir Edmund Chambers attributes to his 'Hand B' and which he sees 'no obvious reason for not assigning to Peele', I find 'No more can I be severed from your side than can yourself yourself in twain divide',[5] I require a great deal more evidence to convince me that the lines are not Shakespeare's.

It is not confined to individuals. Anything which is capable of being personified may be presented as an antithesis in which the two parts are identical; a contradiction in terms, as in 'And Time doth weary Time with her complaining'[6] or 'And Tyranny strike terror to thyself'[7] (the latter again from 'Edward III'). 'Light seeking light doth light of light beguile'[8] in 'Love's Labour's Lost' is merely an elaboration of another line in 'Edward III'—'With light to take light from a mortal eye'.[9] Here it is merely playful, but there are many passages where it is impossible to regard it as a literary conceit, and we are compelled to recognise it as a rudimentary form of casuistry, a method of breaking down the fundamental meaning of words, 'setting the word itself against the word',[10] like Richard II in prison. That

---

[1] *Edward III*, I. 2. [2] *Edward III*, II. I. [3] *Edward III*, I. 2.
[4] *Edward III*, II. I [5] *1 Henry VI*, IV. 5. [6] *R. of L.*
[7] *Edward III*, v. [8] *L.L.L.*, I. I. [9] *Edward III*, I. 2.
[10] *Richard II*, v. 5.

28

play gives us a striking example in the scene where York reveals to Bolingbroke the details of his son's conspiracy, and his wife argues that he is not to be trusted since 'Love loving not itself none other can'.[1] (For the contrary see the sonnet on Self-Love: 'Love so self-loving were iniquity'.) York tells Bolingbroke to say *Pardonne moy* instead of 'Pardon' and she retorts that 'thou dost teach Pardon pardon to destroy' and 'set'st the word itself against the word'. In the New Cambridge edition Professor Wilson tells us that the second line is part of the old play which Shakespeare was revising—'Thyself thyself revisest' in fact!

There is scarcely one of the early plays in which we do not find a character being argued out of an oath. The classical example is, of course, in 'King John', where Cardinal Pandulph argues altogether too forcibly in the form of the contradiction in terms. Philip, according to him, 'makes faith an enemy to faith', swearing against religion, 'by what thou swear'st against the thing thou swear'st', which is 'in thyself, rebellion to thyself'; and his only hope of salvation, since 'fire cools fire' and 'falsehood falsehood cures' lies in being twice forsworn.[2] In Edward III' there are no less than three scenes in which the argument hinges about a breach of faith. Warwick decides to break the oath he has sworn the King for the same reason which the Cardinal suggests to Philip, because it is a contradiction in terms.

> Well may I tempt myself to wrong myself
> When he has sworn me by the name of God
> To break a vow made in the name of God.[3]

I feel that nobody who compares these two passages can possibly doubt that they were written by the same man and more or less in the same mood.

[1] *Richard II*, V. 3.   [2] *King John*, III. I.   [3] *Edward III*, II. I.

But the most striking example of the contradiction in terms is expressed in the idea of Death. Put in the form of the preceding examples the proposition is something like 'Death destroys Death'; that is to say: all we know of death is the fear of it; every time we fear we die, and when we die the fear dies with us, so Death may be said to die too. The corollary is that life is merely a continuance of the fear of Death, so that by seeking life we seek many deaths.

In the early plays and the sonnets we find the proposition in its simple form. 'And Death once dead there's no more dying then';[1] 'The worst is Death and Death will have his day';[2] or 'Fight and die is Death destroying Death'.[3] The remarkable thing is that in 'Edward III' we get the corollary *without* the proposition: 'Since for to live is but to seek to die and dying but beginning of new life.'[4]

It may be that Peele (or Greene) inferred the proposition, though I do not remember any example of it in such work of theirs as I have read, in which case we may also assume that one of them had a hand in 'Julius Caesar' where the corollary is amplified into 'He who cuts off twenty years of life cuts off so many years of fearing death'[5] and 'Cowards die many times before their deaths, the valiant never taste of death but once',[6] and also lent his assistance in 'Measure for Measure' where we are told that 'in this life lie hid moe thousand deaths' and Claudio, like the Black Prince, finds that 'To seek to live I find I seek to die and seeking death find life',[7] and the Duke tells us that 'That life is better life past fearing death than that which lives to fear'.[8]

But surely, again it is quite obvious to anyone reading the two passages on Death which follow, the one from 'Edward III', the other from 'Measure for Measure', that they were written by the same man.

[1] *Sonnets*, 146. [2] *Richard II*, III. 2. [3] *Richard II*, III. 2.
[4] *Edward III*, IV. 4. [5] *Julius Caesar*, III. 1. [6] *Julius Caesar*, II. 2.
[7] *M. for M.*, III. 1. [8] *M. for M.*, V. 1.

For from the instant we begin to live
We do pursue and hunt the time to die.
First bud we, then we blow, and after seed,
Then presently we fall; and as a shade
Follows the body so we follow death.[1]

Merely thou art death's fool;
For him thou labour'st by thy flight to shun
And yet run'st towards him still.[2]

In 'Edward III' the fear of death is itself treated as a
contradiction in terms, because it is in fact a source of
danger. 'If we do fear, with fear we do but aid the thing
we fear to seize on us the sooner,' so that fear too destroys
itself.

The spirit of fear that feareth nought but death
Cowardly works confusion on itself.[3]

Or as the Bishop of Carlisle in 'Richard II' puts it:

To fear the foe since fear oppresseth strength
Gives in your weakness strength unto your foe.[4]

And so, too, Lucrece in the poem:

Mine enemy was strong, my poor self weak,
And far the weaker with so strong a fear.[5]

That 'Edward III' is all Shakespeare's is unquestionable;
that it was written shortly after 'Richard III' and before
'Richard II' and roughly at the same time as 'The Rape of
Lucrece' is highly probable. Its anti-Scottish sentiments

[1] *Edward III*, IV. 4. [2] *M. for M.*, III. 1.
[3] *Edward III*, IV. 7. [4] *Richard II*, III. 2. [5] *R. of L.*

would be fully sufficient to account for its exclusion from the Folio. If I am wrong in believing that 'The Rape of Lucrece' is an artistic treatment of the situation described in the Dark Lady sonnets, then the coincidence that Shakespeare should write such a poem before the situation occurred becomes phenomenal, since in 'Edward III' he not only treats the same situation with obvious biographical detail such as Lodowick's writing of sonnets for the King, but actually uses the proverb on which the Dark Lady sonnets are based. I have no belief in either coincidence, and feel certain that 'The Rape of Lucrece' and 'Edward III' both spring from the same emotional experience as the sonnets, and accordingly conclude that the experience was over and done with by the end of 1593, and that it was to this experience that the poetaster of 'Willoughby's Avisa' referred when in the summer of 1594 he described the 'old player', 'W.S.' as 'newly recovered' from the infection.

IV

THE antithesis of the reflexive conceit seems to have satisfied some fundamental contradiction in Shakespeare's own nature, because all through the sonnets I am conscious that he is doing with the personal situation exactly what he is doing with the words. He is breaking down the terms. I do not mean only those sonnets in which he openly uses the conceit; 'Thou of thyself thy sweet self dost deceive'[1] and 'That 'gainst thyself thou stick'st not to conspire',[2] I mean principally those in which he identifies the lady and the friend with himself, and himself with both; the same identification we find in 'The Comedy of Errors' and 'The Two Gentlemen of Verona'.

He asks the Dark Lady:

> Can'st thou, O cruel, say I love thee not
> When I against myself with thee partake?[3]

This is the same thing which he says to the Friend.

> O how thy worth with manners may I sing
> When thou art all the better part of me?
> What can mine own praise to mine own self bring,
> And what is't but mine own when I praise thee?[4]

Within a short time he is suspecting the Friend of unfaithfulness and using precisely the same conceit.

> When thou shalt be disposed to set me light
> And place my merit in the eye of scorn
> Upon thy side against myself I'll fight,
> And prove thee virtuous though thou art forsworn.[5]

[1] *Sonnets*, 4. [2] *Sonnets*, 10. [3] *Sonnets*, 149. [4] *Sonnets*, 39. [5] *Sonnets*, 88.

Then the Friend becomes the lover of the Dark Lady, and we get it again.

> Thy adverse party is thy advocate
> And 'gainst myself a lawful plea commence.[1]

At the same time he applies the formula to the Dark Lady, and on the ground that the Friend is also himself, half jocosely, half sentimentally consoles himself with the idea that since she loves his Friend 'she loves but me alone'. To admit any blame, the reflexive conceit must be duplicated and negate itself, making a typical bit of early Shakespearean logic, quite gaga but perfectly lucid.

> Then if for my love thou my love receivest,
> I cannot blame thee since my love thou usest,
> But yet be blamed if thou thyself deceivest
> By wilful taste of what thyself refusest.[2]

Only a fool could imagine that this was all jocosity. It is much more like a description of a nature in rebellion against itself. It is Antipholous of Syracuses 'Call thyself, sister, sweet, for I am thee';[3]Valentine's 'Sylvia is myself, banished from her is self from self'.[4] It is the theme of the Marriage sonnets 'That 'gainst thyself thou stick'st not to conspire'; the cry of Richard before the rebel lords: 'I find myself a traitor with the rest';[5] it is the Bishop of Carlisle's warning of the dangers of civil war, 'O if you raise this house against this house';[6] it is Cardinal Pandulph's argument against the King that he has done something which is 'in thyself rebellion to thyself'.[7] It is the overflow of an excessive sensibility which naturally dramatises itself as its own

---

[1] *Sonnets*, 35.   [2] *Sonnets*, 40.   [3] *C. of E.*, III. 2.   [4] *T.G.V.*, III. 1.
[5] *Richard II*, IV. 1.   [6] *Richard II*, IV. 1.   [7] *King John*, III. 1.

opposite; 'the overflow of good converts to bad',[1] a favourite
aphorism of Shakespeare's which dominates 'Richard II'
almost as much as the reflexive conceit itself.

Take one final example from the noble sonnet on Self-
Love ('the most inhibited sin in the canon') with its profound statement of the narcissism which is at the base of all
Elizabethan life and art, and notice how the love of self, to
evade the contradiction in itself, is diverted outward (the
opposite of the contradiction in 'Richard II'—'Love loving
not itself none other can').

> But when my glass shows me myself indeed,
> Beated and chopped with tanned antiquity,
> Mine own self-love quite contrary I read,
> Self so self-loving were iniquity.
> 'Tis thee, myself, that for myself I praise,
> Painting my age with beauty of thy days.[2]

Is it not certain that at this point Shakespeare, from mere
jocosity, has worked down to a fundamental contradiction
in his own personality; an egotism so over-weening that it
transcends itself and becomes abnegation; that this is the
cracking of the shell, the splitting of the personality by
which Richard III becomes Richard II and Aaron Shylock;
Falstaff the hero and Prince Hal the butt? At this period
I feel in Shakespeare a dualism which is almost neurotic;
as though he might quite easily have walked into a room and
found himself sitting there. To me it is as though at last
the antithesis has become flesh; *I* does not cease to think
and feel with the same blind human passion; but on the
very summit of frenzy, *I* suddenly becomes *you* and between them a universe is born.

That change can be immediately perceived in the half
dozen plays which follow: the three 'learned' comedies,

[1] *Richard II*, v 3.   [2] *Sonnets*, 62.

'The Comedy of Errors' (written at some time before Christmas, 1594), 'The Two Gentlemen of Verona' and 'Love's Labour's Lost', with their companion histories, 'Edward III' (1593–4), 'Richard II' and 'King John'. Apart from the certainty regarding 'The Comedy of Errors' I know of no method of assigning dates to these plays or determining in what order they were written. They form one group; all done with great care, and the spidery, almost old-womanish neatness of the sonnet period, but my impression is that 'Richard III', 'Edward III' and 'Richard II' were written in that order, at a lick, and almost without an interval.

It may be only a fancy that the earliest of all is 'Love's Labour's Lost', which is the last word in literary artifice. Sir E. K. Chambers dates it 1595; Professor Wilson, 1593.

The play bears clear evidence of having been revised. The most interesting effect of this has been a change in the last act. The Quarto prints at the end of the play the mysterious words 'The words of Mercury are harsh after the songs of Apollo', to which the Folio adds the still more mysterious 'You that way; we this way.' Of the first Professor Wilson can only suggest that it 'may conceivably have been a comment on the play by someone to whom he (Shakespeare) had lent it for perusal'. What it means is, I think, that originally, the clowns and comedians ended their little masque and sang their two charming songs before the entry of the ambassador, Mercade. 'The words of Mercury are harsh after the songs of Apollo' is the entry line for an ambassador. The play then ended with the separation of the pairs of lovers—'You that way; we this way'—but this wistful, inconclusive ending was disliked by the audience, so, exactly as another hand did with the last scene of 'Troilus and Cressida' Shakespeare broke up the masque by the quarrelling of the comedians in order to give them a re-entry at the end of the play, which thus closes on a happier note.

Apparently it is immensely topical, and the allusions have been read as a light-hearted criticism of the academy established in his home by Sir Walter Ralegh under the tutorship of the astronomer, Harriot. Ralegh himself is supposed to be caricatured as Armado; Nashe as Moth; Chapman or Gabriel Harvey as Holofernes. Undoubtedly, the members of this group, Lord Strange and Sir George Carey were people Shakespeare may reasonably be supposed to have been friendly with, though I am quite certain that neither Ralegh nor Harvey is hinted at in any way; the first because it would not have been safe; the second because a vindictive man like Harvey who was fully aware of everything that went on in literary London would never have written of Shakespeare's work as he did if there had been any question of his having been guyed. The only topical reference which has been identified with anything approaching certainty is that in Holofernes' 'Of piercing a hogshead!'[1] which is generally accepted as an echo of 'Piers Penniless' and Harvey's gibe about piercing a hogshead. 'She knew what she said that entitled Piers the hogshead of wit: Penniless the tosspot of eloquence: and Nashe the very inventor of asses. She it is that must broach the barrell of thy frishing conceit, etc.'[2] Undoubtedly Shakespeare was interested in this controversy because there are other echoes of it in his work, but I am not certain that the jokes about 'piercing' and 'purse' and 'hogshead' would not have been equally topical during the Marprelate controversy, particularly after the appearance of 'Ha' Ye Any Work for a Cooper?' which gave rise to many jokes about tubs and hogsheads. The joke about Judas hanging himself on an Elder would certainly refer better to that controversy as

[1] *L.L.L.*, IV. 2.   [2] G. Harvey, *Piers' Supererogation.*

37

might the mysterious joke about Holofernes and the Fathers. There is a clear echo of it in:

> . . . the corner-cap of society
> The shape of Love's Tyburn that hangs up simplicity.[1]

Here, the last word should surely be 'impiety', and the reference to the three-cornered cap of Tyburn must mark a contrast with the four-cornered cap of the bishops; or as Lilly puts it: 'There's one with a lame wit which will not wear a four-cornered cap, then let him put on Tyburn which hath but three corners.'[2]

The play deals light-heartedly with a group of young men who forswear love for culture and instantly break their oaths, and gives Shakespeare a magnificent opportunity for indulging his passion for sophistry. The keynote is the word 'forsworn' which rings out in this as in 'King John'; there are masses of logic-chopping and contradictions in terms, and a remarkable identification of the author and the Dark Lady with Berowne and Rosaline. This is beyond question, for though it might have been a coincidence that Rosaline like the Dark Lady is 'a whitely wanton with a velvet brow and two pitch-balls stuck in her face for eyes'[3] and an extreme of coincidence that in the almost contemporary 'Romeo and Juliet' Romeo should be 'stabbed with a white wench's black eye'[4] also belonging to a lady called Rosaline; no comic dramatist, unless he were indulging in a private joke, would ever deliberately have destroyed his heroine's character as Shakespeare does Rosaline's:

> Ay, and by Heaven, one that will do the deed
> Though Argus were her eunuch and her guard.[5]

---

[1] *L.L.L.*, IV. 3.   [2] Lilly, *Pap with a Hatchet*.   [3] *L.L.L.*, III. I.
[4] *Romeo*, II. 4.   [5] *L.L.L.*, III. I.

This is very like the writing of a man who knows the girl and her friends are in the theatre.

But all the comedies have echoes of the Dark Lady Tangle. The identification of the poet with the Friend which is the theme of the personal sonnets is repeated in the love scenes of 'The Comedy of Errors' and again in 'The Two Gentlemen of Verona'.

> That thou art then estranged from thyself—
> Thyself I call it, being strange to me.[1]

> As take me from thyself and not me too.[2]

And again we get the echo of 'When thou art all the better part of me'[3] in:

> It is thyself, mine own self's better part.[4]

Apart from a few passages, says one editor, 'it might have been written by anybody', though 'anybody' here must, I feel sure, refer to the actor who, according to Dowden, wrote the vision scene in 'Cymbeline'. If Anybody can produce evidence of his identity he may be certain of a substantial cheque on account from any theatre in the world. 'Errors' is a brilliant adaptation; as in 'The Taming of the Shrew' the cutting in of the sub-plot is achieved with dazzling skill; the skill of the young genius for whom literary creation is still an affair of doing things better than anyone has ever done them before. The play is full of lovely clean strokes of comedy like 'God and the ropemaker bear me witness that I was sent for nothing but a rope',[5] and from few of Shakespeare's plays do I get the same feeling that I can hear the writer's own happy laughter as he wrings another squeeze from the dramatic blue-bag.

[1] *C. of E.*, II. 2.   [2] *C. of E.*, II. 2.   [3] *Sonnets*, 39.   [4] *C. of E.*, III. 2.
[5] *C. of E.*, IV. 4.

39

What one may say in criticism is that it is unsuited to the Elizabethan stage and probably more effective in our day than it was in Shakespeare's The Elizabethan actors, sealed off by the audience like boxers or fencers, were their own background, props and lighting. Since in art every liberty implies a restriction, the poet had to shift his scenery and lighting as frequently as a film producer. The platform stage, like the screen, demanded a certain apparent casualness: it made its effects by a series of brief scenes, all with a slight air of inconsequence as though they were not material, and by sharp, poetic contrasts of night and dawn, woodland and town, passion and farce, trailing into one another without a break. A man walks across the stage exchanging a few gloomy reflections with his brother; a group of carters whom we have never seen before and will never see again chatter in the inn-yard about the absence of chamber-pots. It is a mistake in reading Tudor plays to seek for qualities they haven't got; a grievous mistake to imagine that 'Richard II' improves, or ever was intended to improve, upon the haphazard structure of the chronicle. Chronicle is the essence of the matter.

'The Two Gentlemen of Verona' ought to be a more interesting play than it is, as, quite apart from the recollections of the sonnets such as we found in 'The Comedy of Errors' it has a distinctly personal note. It must be almost contemporary with 'The Comedy of Errors' for it is shaped exactly like it, and though romantic in content, has the same urbane lack of romantic colour. It may be based on an older play from the repertory of the Queen's Players, but, at another remove, is certainly based on the story of Felix and Felismena in Montemayor's endless and pointless romance of 'Diana in Love'. In that story, Felismena, the Julia of the play, is courted through her maid by Felix (Shakespeare's Proteus). Felix goes away and Felismena follows him, disguised as a boy. She puts up at an inn in the town where she knows him to be, but does not know how she is to meet him. Late that night she is summoned by her landlord to listen to a serenade which is being given to the Lady Celia (Shakespeare's Sylvia) and recognises the voice of her faithless lover's serving-man. Later, she becomes his page and courts Celia on his behalf. Celia, like Olivia in 'Twelfth Night', falls in love with her and dies as a result. Felismena takes to the road again, and, after many adventures, finds a man being attacked by several knights, and, going to his rescue, discovers it is Felix. He is properly repentant and marries her.

The later development of the plot was abandoned by Shakespeare as it did not suit the sub-plot which he tagged on to it. His Proteus deceives not only Julia, but his friend, Valentine, who is Sylvia's (Celia's) sweetheart. If one accepts at all the view that there is a factual basis for the sonnets (and I see no way of getting round it), one is bound to recognise that the sub-plot identifies Proteus with the Tarquin of the Dark Lady sonnets—the *third* literary work in which Shakespeare went over the ground—and to spare some sympathy for the unfortunate young nobleman who happened to cross the thin-skinned and exacting poet in his love affair.

In spite of a wretched text the play moves beautifully up to the last act when it goes to pieces. We can only guess what Shakespeare's last act was like, as someone who didn't think it exciting enough, having first cut the play to ribbons, substituted an ending of his own. Valentine in the play is exiled by Sylvia's father, the Duke, who wishes her to marry one, Thurio; and takes refuge with some outlaws among the woods. Sylvia, escorted by the gallant Sir Eglamour, sets out to join him and is pursued by Proteus, Julia (still disguised as a page), Sylvia's father and Thurio. She and her escort are attacked by the outlaws, and Sir Eglamour, no longer gallant, runs away; then she is rescued by Proteus who, finding her at his mercy, decides to rape her, and is finally saved by the appearance of Valentine. At this Proteus repents and Valentine says magnificently, 'All that was mine in Sylvia I give thee'; Julia faints, as well she might, her identity is revealed, and everything ends happily for everybody except the audience, who for two hours have been patiently waiting for somebody to break Proteus' neck.

That the play was cut and the last act botched was shown by Professor Wilson in the New Cambridge edition of the play, and his conclusions seem to me substantially correct. Sir E. K. Chambers does not think that any scenes of incidents have been omitted, but at least one, overlooked even by Professor Wilson, is obvious. In the last scene or the so-called second act we see Julia deciding to dress up as a man and go in search of Proteus. In the second scene of the fourth act (an exceedingly big gap) we find Proteus, Thurio and the musicians ready to serenade Sylvia. There enter two figures, a man and a boy, and the following dialogue ensues, immediately before 'Who is Sylvia?'

—Now, my young guest, methinks you're allycholy: I pray you why is it?
—Marry, mine host, because I cannot be merry.
—Come, we'll have you merry: I'll bring you where you shall hear music, and see the gentleman that you asked for.
—But shall I hear him speak?
—Ay, that you shall.
—That will be music.
—Hark! Hark!
—Is he among these?
—Ay, but peace! let's hear 'em.[1]

From this snatch of dialogue, if we accept Sir Edmund

[1] *T.G.V.*, IV. 2.

Chambers' view, an Elizabethan audience was expected to realise that the boy was Julia, whom they had previously seen only as a woman (a much more serious difficulty then than now as the audience had no means of knowing whether a boy represented a real boy or a girl masquerading as a boy); that she had travelled hither from Verona where they had last seen her; that she had put up at an inn where she had enquired for Proteus, and that the gentleman escorting her was in fact the landlord! All this from a casual 'my young guest' and an equally casual 'mine host'. Even with a cast which needed no doubling and a woman to play the part of Julia it would still be impossible to establish her identity and that of the landlord before the serenade begins. The source shows what has happened: the scene in the inn has been telescoped into the scene under Sylvia's window, and the whole carefully built-up structure of emotion leading to Julia's disillusionment has been demolished.

A glance through 'Diana in Love' shows us how the botcher who telescoped these two scenes must have handled the climax. In the original scenario Sylvia and Sir Eglamour must have been taken prisoner by the outlaws. Then Proteus and Julia must have been attacked, and as in the romance, Julia must have come to the rescue of Proteus. Both would have been saved by the arrival of Valentine and Sylvia, and in explaining his pursuit of Sylvia, Proteus would have been compelled to admit his attachment and endure her reproaches. It may be that at this point Valentine did use the line 'All that was mine in Sylvia I give thee' which is far too close an echo of 'Take all my loves, my love, yea, take them all' to be lightly discarded as an invention of the botcher.

Again, what has happened is that the botcher, having to cut down the play for interior performance, realised that only Sir Eglamour's character stood between him and the possibility of telescoping the two scenes which tied up the two original plots independently, as well as giving the play the added beauty of a projected rape. A man of the theatre with a facility for writing verse could undo a lot of the damage, and I think that careful restoration would show 'The Two Gentlemen' as a play of great charm and a worthy companion-piece of 'The Comedy of Errors'.

When he had written 'Richard III' Shakespeare had come to the end of the York and Lancaster series so far as they could be represented on the stage, and I feel sure that without a break he switched back and began again at the other end with 'Edward III' and 'Richard II'. As I have said, there is no question in my mind that the first two acts of the first play, concerning the courtship of the Countess of Salisbury, were inspired by the Dark Lady episode and are contemporary with the treatment of it in 'The Rape of Lucrece'.

But the contrast with 'Richard III' is startling. The dramatic method is a very rudimentary form of the method Shakespeare was to stick to off and on for the next ten years. He throws over the playboy type of hero exemplified in Richard III. In literature you never find character expressed through pure feeling. By its very nature character is stereoscopic; the focusing of two independent pictures in one. A figure stands out of the page only when there is a certain ambiguity in the writer's approach to him. 'Reality,' in a phrase which Yeats liked to quote, 'is expressed through contradiction.' We can see the direction in which Shakespeare is moving if we compare the wooing of Anne in 'Richard III' with the wooing of the Countess of Salisbury in 'Edward III'. Anne and Richard are cut from the same piece of cloth. It is only by an accident that Anne is the widow of Richard's victim, and she does no violence to her own nature when she becomes Richard's wife. The Countess of Salisbury is a very different person from Edward, and Edward, though like Richard he is willing to wade through rivers of blood to satisfy his desire, is at the same time capable of absurdity, of tenderness, of extreme nobility. We have only to read the exquisite scene when at the height of his love-making, the Black Prince enters, and makes Edward think of the Black Prince's black mother, and for a moment the dream of passion is dissipated.

> I see the boy, O how his mother's face,
> Modelled in his, corrects my strayed desire![1]

Even at the most intense part of the action Shakespeare is not afraid to stand back and poke fun at him. According to Tucker Brooke the play does not contain 'a vestige of comedy',[2] but there are few scenes in Shakespeare so amusing as that in which the King orders his secretary, Lodowick, to write sonnets to the Countess and then rejects the first on the ground that it is inadequate to the subject. This, as I have said, is not only first-rate comedy; it is almost certainly autobiographical.

Unfortunately 'Edward III' is impossible in a modern theatre unless we are prepared to treat the first two acts as an independent play; for they contain an absolutely magnificent part for a star actress whose very existence is ignored after the second act, and scenes equal in power to anything in the great tragedies. No modern audience would tolerate such an anti-climax. But Shakespeare was not writing for a modern audience, but for one whose main interest was in English history, and there is just as much genuine Shakespeare in the history as in the drama.

The most Shakespearean scene of all is that before the battle of Poictiers. The Black Prince's speech, as given by Froissart to Shakespeare, was a typical bit of military rhetoric. 'Now, my gallant fellows, what though we be a small body when compared to the army of our enemies, do

---

[1] *Edward III.*, II. 2. [2] *Shakespeare Apocrypha*

45

not let us be cast down on that account, for victory does not always follow numbers, but where the Almighty God pleases to bestow it', etc. etc. Audley's speech is the same sort of stuff. 'Sir, I have ever served most loyally my lord your father and yourself and shall continue to do so as long as I have life. Dear sir, I must now acquaint you that formerly I made a vow, if ever I should be engaged in any battle where the king your father or any of his sons were, that I should be foremost in the attack, and the best combatant on his side or die in the attempt. I beg therefore most earnestly, as a reward for any services I may have done, that you would grant me permission honourably to quit you, that I may post myself in such wise to accomplish my vow.'[1]

The whole of Shakespeare's mood at this time can be expressed in his treatment of this scene. There was no difficulty about turning Froissart into blank verse; he could do it on his head, and if certain speeches in 'Henry V' can be considered a fair example, he frequently did. Instead, exactly as in 'Richard II', he suddenly withdraws himself completely from the chronicle, and thinking of his beloved contradiction in terms, writes pure lyric poetry.

Prince: Thou art a married man in this distress
         But danger wooes me as a blushing maid:
         Teach me an answer to this perilous time.

Audley: To die is all as common as to live:
         The one inchwise, the other holds in chase;
         For from the instant we begin to live
         We do pursue and hunt the time to die:
         First bud we, then we blow, and after seed,
         Then presently we fall; and as a shade
         Follows the body, so we follow death.

[1] *Froissart Chronicles.*

46

Some supposed borrowings by Daniel from Shakespeare between two editions of his great poem 'The Civil Wars' have caused 'Richard II' to be dated 1595, but since this theory was exploded by Wilson in the New Cambridge edition of the play it is hard to see how Shakespeare's work could have been written *after* the poem, as historically and critically it immediately follows 'Edward III', probably in the spring of 1594. It is a sequel to an excellent play about Thomas of Woodstock, which is probably the work of Shakespeare's friend, Michael Drayton. The characters are still rather stiff; there is a Welsh captain to whom Holinshed's lines on the withering of the bay trees are given, but that is the only thing which shows him a fellow-countryman of Glendower; we meet Hotspur for the first time, but Hotspur is Coldspur. The treatment nowhere compares with Daniel's masterly narrative. In the poem Richard's favourite Norfolk is approached by the popular hero, Bolingbroke, with complaints of the government which Bolingbroke hopes Norfolk will use his influence to remedy. Instead, Norfolk repeats the complaints to the king, and Richard, who takes them as a criticism of himself, confronts Bolingbroke, who returns the accusations on Norfolk. The stage is set for their single combat at Coventry when Richard realises that a victory for Bolingbroke will increase his already dangerous popularity, and, to rid himself of an enemy, sacrifices an ally and exiles both. Instead of this admirable intrigue, Shakespeare has only the empty pageantry of Holinshed.

But half-way through the play there is a remarkable change of mood. The silly ruffian who had taunted an old man on his death-bed becomes in defeat the image of a great man cast down. Here Shakespeare is not merely indulging in the literary acrobatics required by the rather delicate political situation; he is doing exactly what he had done in 'Edward III' and reading into Richard the processes of his own elaborate and very curious mind. In Richard deposed by the rebel lords he sees himself set aside by the Dark Lady and makes him react in an identical way. Because of the contradiction in his own nature Richard is part of what he repudiates. As Shakespeare tells the Dark Lady that 'I against myself with thee partake', Richard tells the rebels:

> Nay, if I turn my eyes upon myself
> I find myself a traitor with the rest.[1]

The identification is complete when we find Richard fascinated by the contradiction in terms which fascinated Shakespeare himself.

> My brain I'll prove the female of my soul,
> My soul the father: and these two beget
> A generation of still-breeding thoughts;
> And these same thoughts people this little world
> In humours, like the people of this world
> For no thought is contented. The better sort,
> (As thoughts of things divine) are intermixed
> With scruples, and do set the Word itself
> Against the word. . . .[2]

It is this which gives 'Richard II' its astonishing quality. Subject and treatment are never fully equated; the emotion portrayed has no full formal equivalent, and the blinding self-pity with which Richard is invested, and which every actor revels in, always transcends the dramatic content and spills over like honey from a pot. The abdication scene is not an abdication but a crucifixion, and if the producer is not to embarrass an audience he must at any cost repress his principal actor.

The method is crude; it is almost a theatrical confidence

[1] *Richard II*, IV. I.   [2] *Richard   II*, V. 5.

48

trick, but it comes off, and in doing so makes the rest of Elizabethan tragedy look like the hope of orphans and un-fathered fruit. What it does in practice is to lower the key of tragedy by several pegs (all poets tend to key tragedy too high) and to bring tragic poetry within Shakespeare's lyric compass. One can immediately detect the difference in quality. This is verse in which the meaning of the words has been sifted, in which Shakespeare has 'set the Word itself against the word'. No one really wants to know the meaning of the adjectives in lines like 'The gaudy, blabbing and remorseful day' or 'To find the empty, vast and wander-ing air' or 'Of the old, feeble and day-weary sun'. They are aimed at the midriff, not at the head. It would seem as though Shakespeare had not yet reached the point of Mercutio's Queen Mab speech in 'Romeo and Juliet' or even Berowne's Women and Learning speech in 'Love's Labour's Lost' for their feathery, idiomatic, prosaic light-ness of touch depends on a characterisation which is still absent from 'Richard II', but you can see how the pitch has been lowered between

> Who raught at mountains with outstretched arms
> And parted but the shadow with his hands

and Richard's speech as he looks in the mirror:

> A brittle glory shineth in this face,
> As brittle as the glory is the face.[1]

You can feel it again between the noble rhetoric of Warwick's dying speech:

> My parks, my walks, my manors that I had
> Even now forsake me, and of all my lands
> Is nothing left me but my body's length.[2]

[1] *Richard II*, IV. 1.   [2] *3 Henry VI*, V. 2.

And the pathos of Richard's with its tremulous repetitions, first indications of the mature style:

> And my large kingdom for a little grave,
> A little, little grave, an obscure grave.[1]

Probably you can feel it best in the difference between two almost identical lines; one from 'Henry VI, Part 3', the other from the play we are considering. When York is captured after the battle near Wakefield, Queen Margaret puts him standing on a molehill, wearing a paper crown, and thrusts into his hand a handkerchief steeped in his son's blood. 'Now looks he like a king' she snarls.[2] When Richard II in defeat appears on the battlements of Flint Castle, York murmurs in almost identical words 'Yet looks he like a king.'[3]

One can feel the stereoscopic effect of the second line, the way in which it makes Richard stand out from his background and fills the stage with air and light. We no longer feel ourselves suffocated in the claustrophobic subjectivity of the 'Henry VI' plays. The images are not so big, but they are in focus; the voice is not so powerful but it is in tune, and it is the sweetest voice in literature.

Why, having written two parts of the new historical sequence, Shakespeare should have interrupted it to write 'King John', or why he should have lingered some years before continuing it I cannot imagine, unless that for all its delicacy, 'Richard II' was too close to the political knuckle. The general belief that he wrote 'King John' to replace the violently anti-Catholic 'Troublesome Reign' which would have been bound to offend Southampton and Strange is probably correct. Professor Wilson argues that it is a revision made in 1594 of an earlier play, basing his

---

[1] *Richard II*, III. 3.   [2] *3 Henry VI*, I. 4.   [3] *Richard II*, III 3.

conclusions mainly on a standing crux in the text. In iii. 4. 68 King Philip's reference to Constance's disordered hair provokes her to reply irrelevantly 'To England if you will.' Both Professor Wilson and the Arden editor assume that this is an ironic reply to an earlier line of his 'I prithee, lady, go away with me' and assume that what lies between the two is an interpolation; but in fact the line does not belong to Constance at all and the printer set it here in error. It is really the last line of the scene: Lewis' reply to the Cardinal's 'For England, go!'

'King John' is merely a retailoring of 'The Troublesome Reign of King John', an old play of the Queen's Men, and Professor Wilson believes that Shakespeare worked on a prompt copy, perhaps brought by himself from the Queen's Men by whom he may have been employed. Shakespeare certainly did not work from a prompt copy of the play, nor could he have been a member of the Queen's Men at any time when it was in their repertory. The printed play contains two separate and mutually contradictory versions of the 'discovery' of Philip, the Bastard. In the original version which the compositor placed second, Philip merely asks his mother:

> Then, madam, thus; your ladyship sees well
> How that my scandal grows by means of you
> In that report hath rumoured up and down
> I am a bastard, and no Faulconbridge.

The second version, placed first by the compositor, is one of the greatest things in English dramatic literature. In this, the two Faulconbridge brothers, Philip the elder and Robert, are arrested for rioting, and, accompanied by their mother, are brought before King John and Queen Eleanor. Philip in his manly way refuses to plead in a matter concerning his mother's honour, whereupon Robert accuses him

51

of being a bastard and incapable of inheriting the family estate. Asked whose bastard, Robert confesses that he believes Philip to be the son of Cœur-de-Lion. Cœur-de-Lion spent much time at their home in the absence of his father; Philip arrived *six* weeks before his time; his appearance answers for the rest. Angered by the charge against their kinsman, both the King and Queen Eleanor take up the cudgels for Philip, declare that no proof has been offered, and in spite of Robert's protests the King decides that he will be satisfied by a mere declaration from Lady Faulconbridge and Philip. Lady Faulconbridge then declares that Philip is her husband's rightful son; Philip himself begins to do so, but suddenly realising the great blood he is forswearing refuses to make the declaration and abandons all claim on the estate, whereupon he is knighted by the King and accepted by him and Queen Eleanor as Cœur-de-Lion's son.

This magnificent scene, masterly in its part-writing, its timing and its mounting tension, is quite complete in itself, but as placed by the compositor with the scene between Philip and his mother immediately following it, it is certainly puzzling. Shakespeare, baffled by the inconsistency, and lacking a proper training on Shakespearean texts, assumed that Lady Faulconbridge's presence in the scene before the King must have been a mistake. Accordingly he deferred her entry until after the actual knighting, thus sacrificing the tremendous effect of her perjury. In her absence, the element of reasonable doubt which is the mainspring of the drama disappears, so he also altered the six weeks of the original to fourteen which is absurd. As a result he made hay of the episode. For all the brilliance of his writing, he never for an instant gets within miles of the inspiration of his predecessor, whoever he may have been.

The weakness of 'King John' is not that it is a mere chronicle play, but that, apart from Faulconbridge, it is not a very interesting one. Faulconbridge's part, however, is fascinating. Here—and also, I suspect, in the part of Berowne in 'Love's Labour's Lost', though this might be considered a junior lead—we have the beginning of a series of character parts for an actor of extraordinary temperament with a considerable gift for mimicry. They range through Berowne, Faulconbridge, Mercutio and Gratiano to Hotspur. The type remains fixed; the bluff, breezy critic of worshipful society, the hater of ceremony and poetry talk, always with a contemporary extravagance spitted on his rapier's point.

> 'A can carve too and lisp: why, this is he
> That kissed his hand away in courtesy;
> This is the ape of form, Monsieur the nice
> That when he plays at tables chides the dice
> In honourable terms. . . .[1]

The pox of such antic, lisping, affecting fantasies, these new tuners of accents: 'by Jesu, a very good blade, a very tall man, a very good whore!'[2]

> 'My dear sir,'
> Thus leaning on my elbow I begin,
> 'I shall beseech you'—this is Question now,
> And then comes Answer like an Absey book:
> 'O sir,' says Answer, 'at your best command;
> At your employment, at your service, sir.'[3]

> There are a sort of men whose visages
> Do cream and mantle like a standing pond,
> And do a wilful stillness entertain
> With purpose to be dressed in an opinion

[1] *L.L.L.*, V. 2.   [2] *Romeo*, II. 4.   [3] *King John*, I. I.

Of wisdom, gravity, profound conceit,
As who should say 'I am Sir Oracle,
And when I ope my lips let no dog bark.'[1]

Heart, you swear like a comfit-maker's wife! 'Not you
in good sooth!' and 'As true as I live' and 'As God shall
mend me' and 'As sure as day'.[2]

It is with him that we first get the Shakespearean soliloquy; a form which, so far as I know, is peculiar to Shakespeare. It is usually only faintly dramatised, or in the
Queen Mab speech or Hamlet's meditation on Suicide not
dramatised at all. It corresponds to the Aristophanic
Parabasis; a personal appearance; a piece of simple essay
writing or a solo on whatever subject happened to interest
the author at the time.

It is fascinating to study how the carefully observed
humours of the Mercutio type loosen the texture of the
blank verse, setting it swaying and spiralling till its fluidity
rivals the sinuous line of the later prose. And I cannot help
wondering if the brilliant character actor for whom the
parts were written was not Shakespeare himself.

[1] *M. of V.*, I. I.   [2] *I Henry IV*, III. I.

V

With 'Romeo and Juliet', 'A Midsummer Night's Dream' and 'The Merchant of Venice' we reach the period of the great masterpieces.

'Romeo' is a betwixt and between play, of a rather curious kind, which at one end approximates less to the lyrical plays than to the earlier 'Richard III' and at the other even surpasses the maturity of 'The Merchant of Venice'. The reason may be that it was revised more than once. Of the textual disturbance in at least two scenes I am not competent to judge, but it is obvious that between the first and second quarto there was some rewriting; the marriage scene has been entirely rewritten, and the dying Mercutio (probably rightly) has been shorn of some of his bitter puns: I regret the loss of his proposed epitaph—

Tybalt came and broke the Prince's laws
And Mercutio was slain for the first and second cause.

But the real test for a literary man is the obviously archaic style of some scenes and the equally obvious mastery of others. Never did undergraduate so dreadfully display his ingenuity as Shakespeare does in the delighted dissection of lines like 'Beautiful tyrant, fiend angelical'; 'Come Montague for thou art early up to see thy son and heir now early down' or the ghastly 'This may flies do while I from this must fly'. As in the Henry VI group we get the heaping up of useless words as in 'Beguiled, divorced, wronged, spited, slain', and we seem 'to hear the lamentations of poor Anne' in the Nurse's 'O woe, O woeful, woeful, woeful day', which rivals anything in the dramatic line of Bottom the weaver. On the other hand, there is the infallible sign of maturity we find in the love scenes; the length of the poetic phrase. In Mercutio's Queen Mab speech, using only his half voice, Shakespeare can produce marvels of delicacy and sweetness, but no momentary inspiration could account for the faultless phrasing of the full concert voice.

> O speak again, bright angel, for thou art
> As glorious to this night being o'er my head
> As is a winged messenger of heaven
> Unto the white-upturned wondering eyes
> Of mortals that fall back to gaze on him
> When he bestrides the lazy puffing clouds
> And sails upon the bosom of the air.[1]

I think that here, as certainly in 'The Merchant of Venice', the main influence on his work is Marlowe's. One whole scene in 'The Merchant of Venice' is cribbed directly from 'Tamburlane'. Marlowe's 'The moon sleeps with Endymion every day', becomes Portia's 'Peace no! the moon sleeps with Endymion.' He has rid himself entirely of his fondness for chop-logic, and, tired of the tight, trim, niggling verse he had been writing, tries for great splashes of colour. In the other two plays of the group the vivid, incantatory classicisms of Marlowe throw a smoky torchlight upon the scene.

> Did'st thou not lead him through the glimmering night
> From Perigenia whom he ravished,
> And make him with fair Aegles break his faith,
> With Ariadne and Antiopa?[2]

Or—from 'The Merchant of Venice'—

> With no less presence but with much more love
> Than young Alcides when he did redeem

[1] *Romeo*, II. 2.   [2] *M.N.D.* I. 2.

> The virgin tribute paid by howling Troy
> To the sea-monster.[1]

Or, once more, from the same play—

> On such a night
> Stood Dido with a willow in her hand
> Upon the wild sea-banks and waved her love
> To come again to Carthage.[2]

Like all actors, Shakespeare had an uncannily retentive ear which could not only recollect a cadence but embalm an error. In 'Soliman and Perseda', which he must have played in in his younger days, there is a line about Juno's goodly swans'—a mistake, for the swans are Venus', not Juno's—but he saved them up for 'As You Like It': 'Like Juno's swans still we went coupled and inseparable.'[3] He must have been a born mimic; he loves to break up his speeches with parody, and has a sort of chameleon quality which makes him seize on any opportunity for a change of style. Those who believe his works were written for him by Marlowe, Greene, Peele, Kyd and Chapman, have plenty of stylistic grounds, for just as in 'A Midsummer Night's Dream' he can cheerfully plunge into a parody of a group of village mummers, he can adapt himself to almost any style. At the same time, being a man of original genius, he never stays adapted.

Even in 'The Merchant of Venice' he does not stay adapted. In the second act there is a scene between two garrulous Venetian merchants, Salarino and Solanio. They describe the frenzy of Shylock after Jessica's elopement in a passage clearly modelled on Marlowe's 'Jew of Malta'— 'O girl! O gold! O beauty! O my bliss!'

> My daughter, O my ducats, O my daughter!
> Fled with a Christian, O my Christian ducats![4]

[1] *M. of V.* III.2. [2] *M. of V.* v. I. [3] *A.Y.L.*, I. 3. [4] *M. of V.*, II. 8.

Then Salarino tells how on the previous day he had met a Frenchman—

> Who told me in the narrow seas that part
> The French and English there miscarried
> A vessel of our country richly fraught.

So far Marlowe's influence. But now we pass to the next scene but one, where again we meet the same two chatter-boxes, but this time talking prose, and again we are informed that 'Antonio hath a ship of rich lading wracked in the narrow seas; the Goodwins I think they call the place, a very dangerous flat and fatal, where the carcases of many a tall ship lie buried'. Shylock appears and we get a characteristic Shakespearean scene of the period with its shattering repetitions—'a beggar that was used to come so smug on the mart—let him look to his bond! He was wont to call me usurer—let him look to his bond! He was wont to lend money for a Christian courtesy—let him look to his bond!' The chatterboxes go off, and to his fellow-Jew, Tubal, Shylock bursts out in a terrific speech, and it is no longer a mere report of what has happened off stage, but the thing itself.

Why there, there, there, there, a diamond gone cost me two thousand ducats in Frankfort—the curse never fell on our nation till now; I never felt it till now—two thousand ducats in that and other precious, precious jewels: I would my daughter were dead at my feet and the jewels in her ear; would she were hearsed at my foot and the ducats in her coffin. . . .[1]

Now, whether or not there was any interval between the writing of these two scenes, you do not have to be a literary

[1] *M. of V.*, III. I.

critic to realise that they are the same scene, and that all Shakespeare has done is to take the hint contained in the Marlovian blank verse and expand it into the prose which by this time was becoming his favourite medium. They make an interesting contrast for they show the direction in which he was moving. Though he might be lured into writing blank verse fantasy his ultimate aim was a closer realism. He refused to stay adapted.

The part of Antonio is the last lingering echo of the Dark Lady episode. As Sir Edmund Chambers and others have pointed out, his melancholy is inexplicable unless we regard it as produced by Bassanio's forthcoming marriage. The melancholy broods over the play which has remarkably little cleverness. For the first and only time Shakespeare in one dangerous line says what Montaigne had already been saying in France—that tortured men will say anything. Was he thinking of Kyd, whose heart-broken preface to 'Cornelia' he must have read?

But the most striking echo of the Dark Lady tangle escapes all the commentators. Bassanio has always been unpopular with them. He has no visible means of subsistence; he borrows money from Antonio, and his only notion of repairing his fortunes is by a wealthy marriage. What they have failed to note is that it is precisely his peculiar, half-lover-like relationship with Antonio which explains his fortune-hunting. They see that Bassanio is a reflection of the young nobleman of the Sonnets but they fail to see that this relationship of rank is also maintained in the play; and that an aristocrat in Bassanio's position could not have done otherwise than seek his fortune in marriage.

I think the distinction in rank has probably been somewhat obscured by re-writing. It is inevitably obscured for the modern reader and playgoer since he is entirely unaware of the light and shade represented for an Elizabethan by ringing the changes on the formal second plural and the intimate second person singular. Whole scenes in Shakespeare have lost their point by our modern inability to detect these changes of key. Half the fun of Malvolio's advances to Olivia is in the fact that he 'thous' her; when Henry V dons Sir Thomas Erpingham's cloak to make his tour of the camp his real disguise is not the cloak but the fact that even when 'thoued' by Pistol he never forgets himself so far as to drop the formal 'you'; when Falstaff accosts the young King on his procession through London his real offence is not that he claims intimacy with him but that he dares to 'thou' him in public, which to any Elizabethan must have seemed like a capital offence. Here, I fancy that a foreigner could probably get more sense from Shakespeare than we can, for on the continent this tradition is still very much alive.

There are two passages in 'The Merchant of Venice' which reveal its significance. In the scene between Antonio and Bassanio the two friends use the formal 'you' for the greater portion of the time. Then Bassanio mentions Portia, and it is as if a quiver of pain runs through Antonio. In his next speech he bursts out 'Thou know'st that all my fortunes are at sea', and the whole scene becomes suffused with emotion. The second is the scene between Antonio and Shylock. Again Antonio uses the formal 'you' until Shylock rates him for his anti-Semitism and Antonio snarls back 'I am as like to call thee so again.'

Anyone who reads the Belmont scenes with care will notice how Bassanio is addressed as 'Your Honour', and though 'thouing' Gratiano (a friend of Antonio), is never 'thoued' by him.

—My lord Bassanio and my gentle lady,
   I wish you all the joy that you can wish,
   For I am sure you can wish none from me:

And when Your Honours mean to solemnize
The bargain of your faith, I do beseech you
Even at that time I may be married too.
—With all my heart so thou can'st get a wife.
—I thank your Lordship, you have got me one.
My eyes, my Lord, can look as swift as yours.[1]

But Antonio is only one part of Shakespeare, the part
that loved a lord. The other is Shylock. Shylock engaged
the real contradiction in his nature, for he is the under-dog
out for revenge. Shakespeare takes great care to confine
his aim to revenge. Though like Barabbas he is the villain
of the play he is never allowed to say the sort of things
Barabbas (or indeed Richard III) says:

As for myself, I walk abroad at night
And kill sick people groaning under walls:
Sometimes I go about and poison wells.

Undoubtedly, Shakespeare has taken great pains to see
that he never becomes a really unsympathetic character:
in us, as in Shakespeare, there is an underdog who has felt
'the insolence of office and the spurns that patient merit of
the unworthy takes', and we know what it is to desire
revenge, even to the extreme of murder. Heine tells the
story of the English girl who sat near him during a performance, and who at the trial scene burst out with 'O, the
poor man is wronged!' That, of course, is the risk which
Shakespeare ran: Shylock, like Falstaff after him, is the
secondary character who steals the play, which tends to
turn into the tragedy of the innocent Jew wrongfully de-
prived of his hard-earned pound of flesh; and it takes the
whole sub-plot of the rings, the serenade and the music to
restore the key of comedy.

[1] *M. of V.*, III. 2.

The greatness of this very great play is that it searches out the Shylock in each of us, and makes us bring in a verdict against judgment and conscience.

'The poor man is wronged.'

VI

SHYLOCK is drawn with careful realism, and as in all the plays of the realistic period, Shakespeare tends to fall back on prose as the subtler instrument, a tendency even more marked in the two parts of 'Henry IV'. But realism is a word we must use with great care. For seven or eight years Shakespeare conceived it his task as an artist to 'hold as 'twere the mirror up to Nature', but he never understood realism as a mere copying of Nature. With him the reflecting medium, whether prose or verse, always came first. Character modifies and enriches it, but is never allowed to replace it, as it frequently does in modern realistic writing. That is to say, Falstaff, Shylock, Benedick and Beatrice are encouraged to speak in their own way, always provided that it is not less striking than Shakespeare's way. 'I will live in thy heart, die in thy lap and be buried in thy eyes; and moreover I will go with thee to thy uncle's.'[1] The phrase is the important thing.

The realistic ambiguity of 'The Merchant of Venice' is nothing to that of 'Henry IV'. Prince Henry is a heroic figure drawn with such asperity that critics have accused him of insensibility; Falstaff a comic ruffian drawn with such lyric tenderness that he steals the play, and whole books have been written to deplore the young King's shabby behaviour in casting him off. 'The poor man is wronged.' One is glad to know that the balance is being redressed by Professor Wilson.

But surely, the important thing to remember is that there is a Falstaff in each of us, and that it is to this Falstaff that Shakespeare appeals. There was certainly a Falstaff

[1] *M.A.N.*, v. 2.

in himself. As I have said in another place, wherever in literature we find those great doubles: Quixote and Sancho, Bouvard and Pecuchet, Daedalus and Bloom, Morell and Marchbanks in Shaw's 'Candida' or Laevsky and Von Koren in Chekhov's 'The Duel', they are never different characters, but different aspects of the same character, usually the author's, and usually externalising a conflict within himself.

When Hotspur cries 'To pluck bright honour from the pale-faced moon!' and Falstaff gloomily asks 'What's Honour?' Falstaff, as Dr. Harrison points out, is guying Hotspur, but even more Shakespeare is guying Shakespeare. Realism is the artistic equivalent of logical thought, and while the poet in Shakespeare revelled in the thought of war, the realist, shrinking from its horrors, was bitterly conscious of the disparity between its causes and effects. One image in particular seems to have haunted him. 'The soldiers,' says Margaret, 'should have tost me on their pikes'; the poor countryfolk of 'Edward III' 'fall numberless upon the soldiers' pikes', while Hippolyta in his last play speaks of 'babes broached on the lance'. And so, in 'Troilus and Cressida' we find the conflict between the young enthusiast, Troilus, and his elder brother, Hector, about Helen of Troy, whose 'youth and freshness', in Troilus' lovely phrase, 'wrinkles Apollo's and makes stale the morning',[1] while to Hector she is merely 'a thing not ours, nor worth to us, had it our name, the value of one ten'. We find the same conflict in 'Hamlet' between the firebrand, Fortinbras, and the philosopher, Hamlet, with his lament for 'the imminent death of twenty thousand men, who for a fantasy, for a trick of fame, go to their graves like beds.'[2]

It is not only Falstaff who asks 'What is Honour?' Shakespeare at the time was asking it too, and, distrusting

[1] *T.C.*, II. 2.   [2] *Ham.*, IV. 4.

64

romanticism, turning away from poetry to prose, and delighting in the bluff violence of his Mercutios and Hotspurs, was in the humour for guying any form of extravagance. In Pistol he indulges in a bout of malicious gibing at the heroic convention in poetry which reveals him in the Cervantes humour, and in the next play he went even further and invented Nym in order to have a fling at the academic realism of Chapman and Ben Jonson.

In 'Henry IV' and 'Henry V' there are two Englands, marvellously balanced; the one romantic, remote, medieval, the other realistic, intimate, prosaic; an England which starts off about its business at dawn with a good grouse at the inn. 'They will allow us ne'er a jordan, and then we leak in your chimney, and your chamber-lie breeds fleas like a loach.'[1] Dramatically, it has little significance; it establishes only the atmosphere; the man awake behind the curtains of the big Tudor bed, watching the lantern flicker on the ceiling and listening to the rustic voices echoing under the wooden posts of the inn-yard. Scholars have pointed out how full these plays are of Cotswold names and places.

This balance, unerringly sustained throughout the first two plays, is magically symbolised in the third when the disguised king visits his troops on the night before Agincourt and learns their views of him. 'As cold a night as 'tis he could wish himself in Thames up to the neck, and so I would he were and I by him.'[2] Realism, which throughout the earlier plays performed the part of bass to the treble of poetry, Mercutio and the Nurse supporting Romeo and his sweetheart, in these plays sweeps up and drowns the note of the violins.

Just as Shylock speaks for the under-dog in each of us, so Falstaff speaks for the average sensual man. In a modern play he would begin every second sentence with 'As a

[1] *1 Henry IV*, II. 1.   [2] *Henry V*, IV. 1.

matter of fact'. The phrase which does identify him like a character in Dickens is 'If I'm not speaking the truth, may I drop down dead!' and on this he continues to ring the changes till the carriers and even the Prince catch it from him, and we see how Shakespeare must have lived the part while writing the play, testing out every phrase with the intonation and gesture of the old man. 'If I fought not with fifty of them, I am a bunch of radish: if there were not three and fifty upon poor old Jack, then am I no two-legged creature.'[1] But like Robin Greene, of whom he frequently reminds me, he is a non-conformist preacher gone wrong; a man once much given to church-going and psalm-singing; and even at his worst he is still full of good resolutions, for to-morrow if not for to-night. 'I must give over this life, and I will give it over; by the Lord, and I do not, I am a villain.'[2] But like the rest of us, he has been swearing the same thing off and on 'any time this two and twenty years'; he does it to the familiar pattern of all his other asseverations, and when the Prince slyly asks where they shall take a purse next day he instantly brightens up and says 'Zounds, where thou wilt, lad; I'll make one; an' I do not call me a villain and baffle me.'[3]

The great trilogy (for I regard 'Henry V' as a third part of the play) is very uneven. The second part, which to judge from its abundance of legal allusions was written for performance at the Inns of Court, is already a decline, and 'Henry V', though it contains magnificent scenes, is a fiasco. Shakespeare must have been badly rattled when he wrote Falstaff's lines in the second part, for he gets nothing right. We scarcely hear the familiar peal of 'An' I do not, call me a villain!' and not once does the old rascal swear to amend his ways. This may do very well for a substitute Falstaff, but it doesn't permit us to identify ourselves with the character—even the poor Civil Servant has hopes of

[1] *I Henry IV*, II. 4.   [2] *I Henry IV*, I. 2.   [3] *IHenry IV*, I. 2.

salvation. Yet, inadequate as he may be, he is still a Hercules of a man, and his total disappearance brings down the curtain.

The mystery of his disappearance from 'Henry V' has never been solved. Professor Wilson accepts the theory that the actor who played the part had left the theatre, and identifies him with William Kempe who certainly did leave the theatre in 1599, the year when 'Henry V' was produced, and whose name Professor Wilson thinks he recognises in an entry for one 'Will' in the Quarto of Part Two. From the parts Kempe is known to have acted I do not see how he could have played the part of Falstaff, and the entry Professor Wilson relies on is clearly for the actor who played Dame Quickly. Dr. Harrison seems to think that Shakespeare had lost the knack of writing about Falstaff, and, seeing how much he had lost grip between the first and second parts, and between the second part and 'The Merry Wives of Windsor', this is a far more likely supposition.

With a purely instinctive writer like Shakespeare it is never safe to push such a question too far; he exhausted a subject or method with extraordinary rapidity, and then left the premises by the window; but my own belief is that he was compelled to drop Falstaff. There was certainly some censorship. Falstaff began as Sir John Oldcastle, but Shakespeare was forced to change the name. It is a reasonable assumption that Lord Cobham, whose family had intermarried with that of Oldcastle, was responsible, since Broome, the name adopted by Ford in 'The Merry Wives of Windsor', was originally 'Brook' (the family name of the Cobhams), and Shakespeare was forced to change that too. Furthermore, while 'Henry IV' was being performed by Shakespeare's company, a whitewashing play, 'Sir John Oldcastle', was produced by the rival theatre, and largesse to the tune of ten shillings (say £5) was distributed among the authors, an item in Henslowe's accounts which always fills me with mild curiosity.

It is quite certain that Shakespeare conceived the plays as a trilogy with Falstaff accompanying the King to France, and that the scene in which the King casts him off, far from being the climax, as so many emotional commentators assume, is merely dramatic preparation for a reconciliation there, 'where for anything I know', as the Epilogue says, 'Falstaff shall die of a sweat, unless already 'a be killed with your hard opinions; for Oldcastle died a martyr and this is not the man.' Curiously, Falstaff does die, and 'of a sweat', but in England, not in France, and his death is merely reported, not shown on the stage.

I may be unduly suspicious, but to my mind there is something very fishy about all this. The impression I get from that magnificent and moving bit of reporting in which we are told of Falstaff's death, is that his part in the third play had already been written, and that Shakespeare was compelled to cut it out. To me the words of the Epilogue 'unless already 'a be killed with your hard opinions' suggest not an appeal for clemency, but, in conjunction with the following clause, 'for Oldcastle died a martyr and this is not the man', a warning to the audience that their belief that Shakespeare had been attacking the memory of a Protestant martyr might make it impossible for him to continue the play as he intended.

Apparently it did, and because of it the play is a failure. 'Banish not him thy Harry's company,' old Falstaff had said, almost as though he already sniffed danger. 'Banish not him thy Harry's company. Banish plump Jack and banish all the world!'

VII

IT was a period of serious change for Shakespeare. Unless 'Measure for Measure' (in its earlier form) intervened, 'Much Ado About Nothing' must have been the last play he wrote for William Kempe. It seems to be a rewriting of an older play since the most important scene required by the scenario is entirely omitted—an unlikely event in a new play. Actually, the reason is that Shakespeare was finding it more and more difficult to adjust his mature realism to the demands made on it by the theatrical conventions of his day, grossly improbable from the realist's point of view, outrageously improper from the moralist's. The main plot of 'Much Ado About Nothing' concerns a girl called Hero, engaged to a young man named Claudio. By some means which in the play is never made quite clear, the villain, Don John, bastard brother of the Duke, arranges that on the night before the wedding Claudio shall apparently see Borachio enter Hero's bedroom. Next morning at the altar he repudiates her, and she is left in a swoon. Her family give her out for dead, and when Borachio is 'reprehended' and the truth emerges, the repentant Claudio is persuaded by Hero's family to marry another girl, who of course turns out to be his own true love, returned from the dead.

The devices which Shakespeare resorts to to make this nonsense palatable are copybook craftsmanship. He attaches a sub-plot of his own devising about a cousin of Hero's, Beatrix, who is a shrew, and a friend of Claudio, Benedick, who is a misogynist, and induces each to fall in love with the other through overhearing that the other is in love with him (or her). That is to say, he attaches a realistic sub-plot, which he writes for all he is worth, and, so far as a dramatist can, diverts the main drama into the new channel he has dug for it. We are not asked to share the highly improbable sentiments of a devoted family keeping Hero concealed; instead we are shown Beatrix eating her heart out with fury at the insult to her friend, egging on Benedick to kill *his* friend. Furthermore, by introducing the clowns as watchmen, and making them 'reprehend' the 'benefactor' of the bedroom plot while he tells an accomplice about it, Shakespeare succeeds in cutting out entirely the most embarrassing scene of the old romance; and by showing us the watch carrying out their investigations in their own enlightened way, he kids us gently along through a couple of enchanting scenes, almost unaware of the abysses of balderdash opening on either hand. It is an absolutely magnificent bit of craftsmanship, and, in spite of the gap in nature left by the missing *scène à faire*, it keeps the old comedy as fresh as a daisy.

At least half the play is carried by the clowns, and that is a risk which Shakespeare could never again have taken, for, in spite of the digs in the pirated version of 'Hamlet', Kempe must have been a superb artist. We seem to trace him from the first skimpy outlines in Costard and Launce to his apotheosis in Dogberry and Pompey Bum. He was obviously the type of melancholy clown who comes on the stage slowly with his trousers hanging down to take the audience into his confidence—in trouble again. He never sees the point of any remark, as his limited acquaintance with the English language causes him to misinterpret and misrepresent everything, and he jogs mournfully on through a series of misunderstandings and malapropisms, wrapped in an impenetrable cloud of conceit until the supreme moment when some misunderstanding no more spectacular than the last induces him to regard himself as insulted. Then his rage is magnificent. 'I am a wise fellow, and which is more, an officer, and which is more a householder, and which is more, as pretty a piece of flesh as any is in

Messina, and one that knows the Law, go to! and a rich fellow enough, go to! and a fellow that hath had losses, and one that hath two gowns, and everything handsome about him: bring him away! O that I had been writ down an ass!'[1] His sudden illuminations are one of his great joys, as when Costard exults in the delicate bawdry of his superiors or Launce flares up after the departure of Speed: 'Now will he be swinged for reading my letter—an unmannerly slave that will thrust himself into secrets.'[2]

But on the whole he is a warm-hearted fellow, and full of sympathy for neighbours who lack the benefits of intellect which 'Fortune' has showered on him. 'Goodman Verges, sir, speaks a little off the matter, an old man, sir, and his wits are not so blunt as God help I would desire they were, but in faith, honest, as the skin between his brows.'[3] 'He is a marvellous good neighbour, faith, and a very good bowler: but for Alisander—alas, you see how 'tis—a little o'erparted.'[4]

He obviously set the key for all the low comedy parts in the earlier plays, for it is not only those clearly written for him like Costard, Bottom, Dogberry and Pompey Bum which exploit his characteristics, but others like Mrs. Quickly which apparently were written for other actors.

These parts form a startling contrast to those for Robert Armin who took Kempe's place in the theatre in 1599. Armin was equally clearly the slick clown who bounces on to the stage with a hop, skip and jump, and a merry cry of 'Here we are again!' Jonson in 'The Poetaster' gives us a partial and unflattering picture of him. 'Your fat fool . . . let him not beg rapiers nor scarves in his over-familiar playing face, nor roar out his barren bold jests, with a tormenting laughter, between drunk and dry. . . . Give him warning, admonition, to forsake his saucy, glavering grace, and his goggle eye: it does not become him, sirrah:

[1] *M.A.N.*, IV. 2.   [2] *T.G.V.*, III. 1.   [3] *M.A.N.*, III. 5.   [4] *L.L.L.*, V. 2.

tell him so.'[1] He had a good voice and could write his own songs. He had an absolute passion for the work of Shakespeare; not so much for the comedy parts, which he probably thought he could do better himself, but for the great tragic roles. Again it is the old story of the clown with the painted face who watches with jealous rage while Hamlet comes off, still lost in the cloud of his passion. When ten years later Armin wrote a play himself it was about a young man whose sensibilities were outraged by his mother's adultery (only apparent this time, one is glad to say). His name was Humil! That preposterous play, 'The Two Maids of Mortlake', is to me the most moving of all Shakespearean documents for it reveals all that the historical documents conceal; the tremendous impact on the imaginations of simple men that was produced by Shakespeare's daily presence: it is like the splashing of waves on the shore after the great ship of literature has sailed silently by.

'As You Like It' (1599) was actually begun for Kempe, 'the roynish clown', and hastily adapted for Armin. The play presented few difficulties except the usual one of the girl in boy's clothes which never troubled Shakespeare since he hadn't seen a real actress. Rosalind is an enchanting bit of part-writing for the quick-tongued lad who had played Beatrix: but apart from her the play is something of a rag-bag. A part has been provided for a mysterious satirist called Jacques who has nothing at all to do, and, like Pistol and Nym, seems to have been dragged in merely to guy some contemporary figure or extravagance. Shakespeare found it impossible to fit Armin in, and his part, like Jacques, remains outside the action and could be suppressed with little damage to the play. He has a mistress called Audrey, a rival called William, and a hedge-parson called Oliver Martext to marry him, but his lines never rise

[1] *Poetaster*, 3. 4. 300.

above the level of deft patter, and they cast a cold deliberate light over the whole play which is absent from its weaker but more human predecessor. 'I press in here, sir, amongst the rest of the country copulatives to swear and to forswear, according as marriage binds and blood breaks: a poor virgin, sir, an ill-favoured thing, sir, but mine own; a poor humour of mine, sir, to take that that no man else will: rich honesty dwells like a miser, sir, in a poor house, as your pearl in your foul oyster.'[1]

The slick, bloodless, homosexual patter refuses to take dramatic colouring like Kempe's robuster buffoonery; nor did Shakespeare ever succeed in dramatising it, for in 'Twelfth Night' and 'All's Well That Ends Well' Armin remains the court clown. Contrary to the usual view, I feel that the former play is again a decline on 'As You Like It'. It is, of course, excellent theatre, but the lyric quality is fitful and slight, and Armin's icy slickness invests all the characters in an impenetrable armour of allusiveness. The compositor probably added to this because I cannot help feeling that Sir Toby's 'My lady's a Cataian; we are politicians'[2] does less than justice to Olivia's character; I fancy Shakespeare meant her to be a 'Catonian' (i.e., My lady's a woman of principle; we are opportunists). The weakness is the weakness of all cleverness: the glassy surface, the lack of interior perspective. The epigrams, all to one tune, are rolled off suavely like those in a Wilde play, but though one thinks of the epigrams themselves one never thinks of who said them or in what connection. Gilbert guyed them neatly in his 'I would as lief be thrust through a quicket hedge as cry Pooh to a callow throstle.' Only in 'Lear', where the peculiarly eerie quality of cleverness gives it a sort of ghostly music, does Shakespeare get near dramatising it. So far as I recollect, malapropism as a source of fun practically disappears from the plays, and

[1] *A.Y.L.*, v. 4.   [2] *T.N.*, II. 3. 77.

its place is taken by patter and repartee; and something of warmth, of kindness, of the poetry of the inn and the village green disappears with it. We no longer hear the music of 'He is a marvellous good neighbour, faith, and a very good bowler.' It is as though the lights were going out in Shakespeare's mind.

I feel that none of the plays of this period really comes off. 'The Merry Wives of Windsor' is a good rough comedy but without a glimmer of distinction. The Fenton and Windsor Park scenes are in a distinctly unShakespearean style, and believers in the transmigration of plays have no difficulty in proving that the soul of his grandam inhabits Falstaff. I suggest that they may be the work of the man who wrote the couplets in 'All's Well That End's Well' and that, instead of being the hypothetical author of Old Plays, he may have been a scenarist who prepared the groundwork for this and other plays.

'Julius Caesar' (1599) is a very strange play in a very strange style. It is purely political and apparently intended to discourage would-be revolutionists by emphasising the lesson of 'Henry IV': 'An habitation giddy and unsure hath he that builds upon the vulgar heart.' On that dubious text Shakespeare could preach till doomsday without a hint of unorthodox, let alone original, thinking: 'preordinance and first decree'; 'the primogenitive and due of birth', 'prerogative and tithe of knees' (the balance of Latin and English synonyms is characteristic of the period) never admits a rival, so that the play is necessarily satirical. In the scene of Mark Antony's speech the satire is brilliant, but satire dragged out for five acts is desperately tiresome, and as if to emphasise this, it is written in a deplorable style. Sir Edmund Chambers, following Bradley, suggests that Shakespeare 'was deliberately experimenting in a classical manner with an extreme simplicity of vocabulary and phrasing', which seems a rather inadequate description

74

of the style. In a very bad text of a very bad play, 'The Massacre of Paris', improbably attributed to Marlowe and apparently produced about 1592, there are two lines: 'Yet Caesar shall go forth' and 'Thus Caesar did go forth and thus he died', which suggests that this piece of clap-trap was then known and popular; Sir Edmund surmises that as the printed play has no date, it may not have appeared before 1599 when the echo of 'Julius Caesar' was introduced. What is certain is that the style of 'Julius Caesar' is the style of 1590, not that of 1599.

> No, Caesar shall not, Danger knows full well
> That Caesar is more dangerous than he. . . .[1]

is typical. The characters all tend to address one another and refer to themselves in the lachrymose third person singular, a trick which Shakespeare with his idiomatic style used sparingly, and which reduces everything to the dead level of 'Little Julie wants a doll'. There is also a superfluity of auxiliary verbs and one wearies of learning how 'I did mark how he did shake' while the oratorical repetitions make us far too conscious of the platform stage and of actors moving in a circle. At the same time, in other plays of the period Shakespeare does show a certain weakness for the third person singular and for auxiliary verbs, even if to nothing like the same degree.

We must leave it at that. The play is undoubtedly Shakespeare's and undoubtedly of this period, and one can only guess that he was revising in an uncritical mood something which he had written at the time of the 'Henry VI' plays, for the only passages of value are those in his own vigorous contemporary style which sometimes breaks through the academic phrasing with startling effect as in 'It is the bright day that brings forth the adder'.

[1] *J.C.*, II. 2.

'Troilus and Cressida', on the other hand, is a brilliant bit of work. It has been variously interpreted as a comedy of disillusionment, an attack on Jonson and Marston, a warning to Essex, and a satire on Chapman's Homer, while some editors lean to the belief that Thersites represents Shakespeare's considered view of human existence as 'Wars and lechery'—though not for long, one is glad to know.

There is, of course, something radically wrong with a play which leaves itself open to such a variety of mis-interpretations, and we can accept it as proved. The main trouble is that for a play with such a title we see far too little of the lovers, and it looks far more like the first part of a history dealing with the fall of Troy. The main problem discussed is why Troy took so long to capture. Like all Shakespeare's political work it is tendentious and satirical, though the characters are much more clearly differentiated than in 'Julius Caesar' and the political thought is on a far higher plane. It is interesting to see Justice treated not as an absolute but as a mean between Wrong and Right; Choice as a mean between Will and Judgment; and as for instance in Nestor's warning that the success or failure of an elected representative has an important effect on the character of the community, the thought is sometimes profound. The language is a development of the stylistic experiment in the great choruses of 'Henry V'. It may be that to write the French scenes in that play Shakespeare had started to read French again, because in quick succession he gives us a number of Gallicisms and semi-Gallicisms like 'rivage', 'sternage', 'vaultage' and 'farced'. As well as this, he seems to have read some metaphysics, and between Gallicisms and Latinisms, the style of 'Troilus and Cressida' frequently degenerates into mere jargon. There is wholesale coinage of words ending in '-ure' and '-ive'; words like 'flexure' and 'tortive'; queer words like 'mirable' and 'convive' and ugly words like 'propugnation' and 'oppugnancy', while even Troilus is bound to become an unsympathetic character when he tells us about

> a credence in my heart
> An esperance so obstinately strong.[1]

But the enduring charm of the play is its suggestiveness. Few plays say less and suggest more. The use of the double plot is brilliant. The disillusionment of Troilus with Cressida is subtly and most movingly harmonised by the growing disillusionment of the warring armies whose great causes have begun to decline into mere personalities, vanities and private attachments. Both armies are affected; the Trojans because though young Troilus, in love himself, believes that honour requires the retention of Helen, his maturer brothers, Hector and Helenus remember the words of Lucrece when she sees the strumpet Helen in the picture of Troy:

> Why should the private pleasure of some one
> Become the public plague of many moe?
> Let sin, alone committed, light alone
> Upon his head that hath transgressed so.[2]

But Shakespeare's main interest lay in the attackers. They are meeting with no success for the usual statutory reasons: 'degree is shaked'; 'the odds is gone'; 'preordinance and first decree', 'the primogenitive and due of birth', 'prerogative and tithe of knees' are, as usual, in a shocking state. The statesmen are at loggerheads with the military leaders, and Shakespeare's treatment of the generals passes all the bounds of satire and becomes mere scurrility. Achilles and Ajax, the first with his effeminate friend Patroclus, are beasts and idiots, who cannot be stirred

[1] *T.C*, v. 2.   [2] *R. of L.*

except by appealing to their vanity and jealousy. Wise Ulysses sees that the only hope of getting Achilles to fight is to set up Ajax as a rival commander. The great plan meets with some success, but finally collapses when Hector refuses to fight Ajax on the ground that he is 'his father's sister's son', while Achilles, subordinating his vanity to his lust, goes to keep an appointment with Polyxena in the enemy's camp! Here the irony is more reminiscent of Voltaire than Shakespeare.

It becomes even more blistering when the problem of the Greeks is settled not by the wisdom of Ulysses but the thoughtlessness of Achilles' boy-friend Patroclus, who gets himself killed by Hector while Ajax's friend loses his life at the hands of Troilus. At this point the generals decide that the thing is going too far and take the field. As Achilles is totally incapable of defeating Hector in fair fight, he has him murdered. This startling scene is the climax of the disillusionment in the under-plot; the harmonic background to Cressida's betrayal of Troilus, which is murder on a different plane; the murder of the heart. The two themes are most ingeniously linked by the clown, Thersites, who is there as chorus on every occasion, even when Cressida is deceiving Troilus with Diomed, and whose comments are always the same—'Wars and lechery! Still wars and lechery!' Editors ask incredulously can this be Shakespeare? Of course, Thersites is a pure O'Casey figure; Shakespeare's reply to the libels of the liberal wits; a satire on the satirists whose perpetual chorus of criticism in his view sapped the state. Ten years earlier, Gabriel Harvey had used Thersites as a symbol for the same thing, and Shakespeare may actually have been thinking of Harvey's words 'But Titius or rather Zoilus in his spiteful vein will so long flurt at Homer, and Thersites in his peevish moods so long fling at Agamemnon that they will become extremely odious and intolerable to all good learning and civil government; and in attempting to pull down or disgrace other without order, must needs finally overthrow themselves without relief.'[1]

Apart from what appears to be a recollection of the Dark Lady episode, I see no personal disillusionment in the play; nothing which links it in my mind with the tragedies that follow, I cannot for the life of me see where Dr. Harrison gets a Troilus who is 'lust-mad' or a Cressida who is 'a whore'. It is a play of the ice-brook's temper, cold and bright like a frosty day, and with none of the Nordic glooms and fogs of the tragedies, but in the light of these I suppose I must be wrong. A great deal of the suggestiveness which gives the play its beauty, must have come of Shakespeare's realisation that the subject itself was dynamite. When the principal object of a writer is to cover up his tracks, it is useless to try and identify contemporary allusions, but surely, at the end of the sixteenth century only a political innocent could have failed to draw a parallel between Ulysses and Nestor, Ajax and Achilles on the one hand and Cecil and Bacon, Essex and Ralegh on the other? I find it impossible to believe that any Elizabethan could have seen (if any Elizabethan *did* see) so vicious a caricature of the military leaders of the Grecian army without thinking of his own military leaders, one of whom, compared by his admirers with Achilles, as Dr. Harrison has shown, sulked in a way distinctly reminiscent of that hero; while the remarkable passage about Ulysses' intelligence service must, I feel, have pointed the analogy to any Londoner. If the play ever was produced, which is very doubtful, it must have been when Achilles-Essex was already a doomed man. This would fully explain its strange eventful history. On February 7th, 1603, it was entered for publication by James Roberts 'as it is acted by my Lord Chamberlain's men' but never published by him. In 1609 it was published by an

[1] G. Harvey, *Four Letters.*

79

entirely different publisher with a statement to the effect that it had never been produced at all. This proves that by that time it had been long dropped from the repertory, if it ever was really in it. What happened after February 7th, 1603, which made it inadvisable either to publish or produce it was clearly the Queen's death on March 24th. Already, in the corresponce between Henry Howard, Earl of Northampton, and James VI, the destruction of Essex's enemies, Ralegh, Lord Cobham, Shakespeare's enemy, and Lord Grey de Wilton, was being prepared. On April 7th (I follow Dr. Harrison's admirable 'Jacobean Journal') Cecil refused to allow Cobham to act as Ralegh's substitute Captain of the Guard. On April 10th, Southampton and Neville, the two survivors of the Essex conspiracy, were released; on April 23rd, on his way south, James I promised the Bishop of Durham, Toby Matthew, to restore the alienated property of his bishopric (Durham House, which Elizabeth had presented to Ralegh). On May 8th, exactly one day after his arrival in London, James dismissed Ralegh from his position as Captain of the Guard; at some time before June 7th he ordered him to quit Durham House. On July 1st, in the presence of the Queen, Southampton insulted Grey de Wilton during an argument about the Essex Rebellion. On July 14th, Ralegh, Cobham, his brother and Grey de Wilton were arrested on a charge of treason, Ralegh's treason being alleged to have taken place on June 9th—long after a babe in arms might have seen he was a doomed man.

It was a bad time for enemies of Essex. Towards the end of May, Shakespeare's company produced Jonson's 'Sejanus'. We have Jonson's own statement that 'Northampton (Henry Howard) was his mortal enemy for brawling on a St. George's Day one of his attenders, he was called before the Council for his "Sejanus" and accused both of popery and treason by him'. The Editors of the Oxford

Jonson suggest that Howard, who was himself a Catholic, attempted to injure a co-religionist in order to conceal his own activities, but I am afraid that Jonson's statement needs to be taken with a grain of salt. The real reason why Howard hauled him before the Privy Council is revealed in a note by Dr. Harrison. 'Ben Jonson, in the margin of his copy of Greenaway's translation of *The Annals* of Tacitus, noted opposite the account of the fall of Sejanus "The Earl of Essex".'[1] Jonson had already attacked Essex in 'Cynthia's Revels' at a time when Essex was a doomed man. Howard was scarcely like to forget that. In the following year Samuel Daniel was also haled before the Council for a slander on Essex. It was certainly not a good time for publishing a play like 'Troilus and Cressida' with all its echoes of the Essex conspiracy.

But apart altogether from this, some of the scenes are miracles of dramatic tact, of the deliberate refusal to underline a situation. We see early in the play that Hector wishes to send Helen back to her husband, Menelaus. Then Pandar, arranging for Troilus to spend the night with his niece, calls to Paris to make Troilus' excuses at supper; Helen rags him; he goes, and Paris asks her to come and unbuckle Hector's armour. She agrees, and as they go out he suddenly throws his arms about her and murmurs 'Sweet, above thought I love thee.' Not by a word has Shakespeare emphasised his fears that Hector may have his way. Remember, too, that unforgettable little scene I have mentioned already when the two brothers Paris and Troilus, the one the happy, the other the unhappy, lover, come to warn Cressida that she must leave the city. They utter just a few lines of verse which almost succeed in expressing the inexpressible. Last of all, consider the scene between Troilus and Hector on the morning of the final battle. Troilus has just had his own bitter experience of Cressida's

[1] *A Companion to Shakespeare Studies*, p. 167.

treachery, Hector is going out to die by Achilles'. By a supreme touch of dramatic irony, this is the moment when the lofty young idealist, Troilus, chooses to reprove his brother for showing pity to the vanquished.

Hector: Oh, 'tis fair play.
Troilus: Fool's play, by Heaven, Hector.
Hector: How now! How now!
Troilus: For the love of all the gods
         Let's leave the hermit pity with our mothers,
         And when we have our armours buckled on
         The venomed vengeance ride upon our swords,
         Spur them to ruthful work, rein them from ruth.
Hector: Fie, savage, fie!
Troilus: Hector, then 'tis wars.[1]

The exploration of the mind of a romantic young man who has experienced his first disillusionment could go no further. And like everything else through this great play it is stated without comment, almost as though its implications had never even occurred to the author.

Dramatic tact could go no further.

[1] *T.C.*, v. 3.

VIII

THE realistic period stops dead with 'Hamlet' (1601–2),
which is a play with two faces. One, with its delightful
portrait of Polonius, as delicate as anything in Jane Austen,
looks back to the lyrical plays; the other with its gloomy
soliloquies and the macabre humour of the Gravediggers'
Scene, written in for Armin, looks forward to 'Othello' and
'Lear'.

It is also a play of two styles. The first is smooth, lucid
and stately; its unit the couplet or extensions of the couplet.

> We do it wrong, being so majestical,
> To offer it the show of violence
> For it is as the air invulnerable
> And our vain blows malicious mockery—[1]

The second is nervous, harsh and vibrant, its unit the
couplet between two half-lines.

> O such a deed
> As from the body of contraction plucks
> The very soul, and sweet Religion makes
> A rhapsody of words
> Heaven's face doth glow
> Yea, this solidity and compound mass
> With tristful visage, as against the Doom,
> Is thoughtsick at the act.[2]

'This solidity and compound mass' is one of the
'dictionary' lines which identify the Shakespeare of the
'Hamlet' period and after: it is a reversion to weight as

[1] *Ham.*, I. 1.   [2] *Ham.*, III. 4.

against grace. The dictionary line became something of an obsession with Shakespeare. In 'Henry V' (1599) he wrote ' 'Tis no sinister nor no awkward claim',[1] than which no more sinister nor more awkward combination seems possible, but the twin of 'sinister' haunted him for years until in 'Sir Thomas More', which must be at least five years later in date, he got in 'To give the smooth and dexter way to me.'[2] Frequently it is as though he *were* working with a dictionary, and testing both the Latin and English form of a word to see which is the better. 'It is a nipping and an eager air.' 'The inaudible and noiseless foot of Time.' 'The primogenitive and due of birth.' But sometimes with a nervous jerk he gives us not the translation but an apparently unrelated word which breaks the logical development with a snap and floods the line with pure association. 'The expectancy and rose of the fair state.'

There was an old play of 'Hamlet', probably by Kyd, but we can only guess what it was like. There is also a German 'Hamlet', unfortunately drastically cut, but whether this is derived from Kyd's or Shakespeare's play is hard to say. Sir Edmund Chambers believes it is merely a corruption of Shakespeare's.

Like Kyd's 'Spanish Tragedy', it opens with a Senecan prologue which is spoken by Night and the Furies. The first scene takes place on the battlements of Elsinore, and unlike 'Hamlet' in which the Ghost appears on two successive nights, the episode is closed in the first scene: the Ghost appears first to Horatio, then to Hamlet, to whom he recounts the story of his murder. Hamlet, interrupted by the Ghost while he tries to repeat the story to his companions, finally tells Horatio only, and explains that he intends to sham madness to get an opportunity of killing his uncle.

Laertes (here called Leonhard) is permitted to go to

[1] *Henry V*, II. 4. 87.   [2] *Sir Thomas More*, III. 2.

France while Hamlet is persuaded to remain at home. He first shams madness before Ophelia, and the King and Polonius (called Corambis) overhear the conversation in which he tells her to 'go to a nunnery'. The Players appear, and Hamlet, having given them some advice on acting, asks them to perform a play about the murder of King (he forgets the name) Pyr-Pyr-Pyrrhus. The Dumb Show only is performed; the King is shocked into betraying himself; Hamlet visits his mother's room and bids her 'look upon this picture and on this', and kills Polonius who has been listening. He is sent to England, and Ophelia goes mad and makes bawdy overtures to a courtier. Hamlet, on his way to England, is attacked by two banditti, and kills both by dropping flat as they discharge their pistols at him. Laertes returns from France, demanding revenge, and Hamlet is killed with a foil poisoned by the King.

Besides this, we have also a shorthand version of Shakespeare's 'Hamlet' pirated by a printer. This is substantially like 'Hamlet' as we know it, but there are two major differences. In this version, in which, as in the German, Polonius is called Corambis, the two scenes, Hamlet-Ophelia and Hamlet-Rosencrantz and Guildenstern are transposed; and instead of the two scenes in which Horatio receives a letter from Hamlet and then discusses his escape with him, we have one scene only in which Horatio tells the Queen of his escape. Sir Edmund Chambers believes that both the German play and this derive from a performance of 'Hamlet' in which, for some reason of prudence, 'Polonius' was changed to 'Corambis', and the two scenes, Hamlet-Ophelia and Hamlet-Rosencrantz and Guildenstern were transposed, though he admits that 'why the change should have been made is not clear'.

To return to the German version. The only serious blot on it is the comic treatment of Ophelia's madness which is usually considered to be the work of the German adapter.

I believe it to be the earliest of the three versions, merely because it is by far the most workmanlike scenario of the three, and I find it hard to imagine that a text can be clarified in corruption. Consider, for instance, the simple matter of the Ghost's repeated 'Swear!' I do not think I am abnormally dense, but until I read the German text I had always taken that for a piece of romantic colour, and never understood that the Ghost was uneasy at the thought of strangers learning the secret of his murder; that Hamlet broke off on his account, but merely deferred repeating the story till later. Of course, from the fact that at the time of the Play Scene Horatio knows the story, we may deduce that Hamlet told him, but why he delayed in telling him is certainly not clear from the play. One line in the German makes the whole thing plain. 'The spirit of my father is perturbed that I should make this matter known.'

Again, the scene of Hamlet's escape from his would-be murderers, however crudely it is treated, is a necessary scene which Shakespeare dropped to his own great confusion. He made two shots at covering up its absence, neither successful. It is not good craftsmanship to make the audience aware of a plot against your hero's life and then bring him back a quarter of an hour later to tell how he escaped it. It is bad craftsmanship when, as in 'Hamlet', the burial of Ophelia has to take place before he can tell the story at all, for by that time Hamlet's existence is taken for granted, and nobody gives a button how he escaped. The much-discussed question of whether or not the King saw the Dumb Show is answered in a rather remarkable way, for it seems that the King saw nothing else. The whole story is simple and clear with none of the redundancies and inconsistencies of Shakespeare's play, though exactly how far this may be accounted for by cutting is not clear. There are no Rosencrantz and Guildenstern, no Marcellus, no Fortinbras except in a casual reference, no grave-diggers, no Hecuba scene—nor, indeed, is there any apparent need for them. The story is pure Deadwood Dick. Perhaps Shakespeare's most miraculous achievement was to take a Deadwood Dick story which the audience knew as well as himself and transform it into one of the great myths of the world.

His method—unsatisfactory from the artistic point of view—was to shift the emphasis. Hamlet of the German play is a Renaissance man of action, bold and cunning; and both the boldness and cunning have left their traces on 'Hamlet', notably in the scene where Hamlet apologises to Laertes almost entirely in the third person singular (as suspicious here as in 'Julius Caesar') and excuses himself on the ground of his supposed madness. Sham madness as a dramatic convention was already as dead as Queen Anne— Shakespeare's Queen Anne. 'It may appear to some ridiculous,'[1] says the sham madman in Webster's play, with a nervous glance at the young gentlemen from the Inns of Court. Shakespeare's Hamlet is an intellectual afflicted with melancholia; so that even if there were no Rosencrantz and Guildenstern in the original play (and I see no reason to think there were), one can see how necessary it would have been to invent them, merely to balance the sham madness which Hamlet assumes before Ophelia and Polonius with the real melancholy which Shakespeare was now trying to graft on him. Notice in particular how before the mad scene with Ophelia he interpolated the great meditation on suicide—clearly interpolated it, because, contrary to the convention of Elizabethan play-writing, the King and Polonius overhear the scene with Ophelia but not the soliloquy. And if you assume as I do that the German version is the earliest of the three, you can see exactly why it was that between the pirated version of 1603 and the official version of 1604, Shakespeare found it so necessary

[1] *The White Devil*, IV. 2.

to transpose the Hamlet-Ophelia and the Hamlet-Rosencrantz and Guildenstern scenes—to correct any false impression and present his audience first with a Hamlet suffering from real melancholia rather than with one shamming madness.

The fundamental inconsistency between the scenario and the treatment is the cause of almost all the muddle in the play. Forgetting the limitations of his Deadwood Dick theme, Shakespeare tends to throw the emphasis too much on the intellectual side, and then is brought up dead by the limitations of the plot. The introduction of Rosencrantz and Guildenstern involves him in a typical difficulty. In the German version the whole thing is plain sailing; the players are strolling mummers; they appear, Hamlet instantly gets the idea of the Play scene and gives them a lecture on acting. But then Shakespeare had the inspiration for the mighty Hecuba scene—probably from the same source as so many other things in 'Hamlet', Montaigne's Essays, for, according to Montaigne, 'Quintilian relates that he saw actors who entered so deeply into a tragic part that they still wept after reaching home; and of himself he tells us that having undertaken to work upon others' feelings he was so carried away by his own that he detected himself not only in tears but with the paleness of countenance and behaviour of a man really overwhelmed with grief.'[1]

Accordingly for the purposes of the scene the mummers become the tragedians of the city (and perish any mummer who adopts Dr. Harrison's suggestion that the scene should be clowned!), on tour because of the vogue of child-actors, and encountered on their way by Rosencrantz and Guildenstern. Now the Advice to the Players is merely in the way of the great scene, so like the mad scene with Ophelia, it has to be pushed back to its present position; but even this doesn't entirely solve Shakespeare's problem, since with

[1] *Montaigne's Essays*, tr. Trechman.

Rosencrantz, Guildenstern and Polonius on the stage, it is impossible for Hamlet to arrange the details of the plot for making the King betray himself, yet, if he doesn't, he leaves the players with no dramatic carry-over. So in spite of the presence of the others Hamlet calls the chief player aside and slips in a few lines about an imaginary speech which he is to write for the play next evening, and to this speech Shakespeare skilfully pegs the now homeless and destitute Advice to the Players. And even this leaves a very awkward moment, for the emotional effect of the Hecuba scene compels Shakespeare to follow up at once with the great monologue on irresolution and reserve the actual detail of the plot, which in the German play, *precedes* the Players' entrance, for the very end of the scene. Only the very suspicious notice that Hamlet has arranged for the speech which he is to write into the play before the idea of the play scene occurs to him at all. He makes the same mistake as when he allows Hamlet to explain his escape after the burial of Ophelia, and for the same reason; that he has interpolated something into the text. It is exceedingly skilful but patchy.

I do not suggest that all the alterations were made at different times; they may represent no more than the ordinary changes of intention visible in the manuscripts of most writers; but some were certainly made between the appearance of the two Quartos, in 1603 and 1604, and I have suggested elsewhere that the whole mysterious Fortinbras business may be an interpolation connected with the old Queen's death and the problem of the succession.

In the very first scene Marcellus asks what is afoot in Denmark, and Horatio (elsewhere referred to as a stranger) explains in a long speech that a Norwegian prince called Fortinbras is raising an army to invade Denmark. Fortinbras appears again a few scenes later when two ambassadors who have no other earthly business in the play are despatched to Norway to protest. Later they return with the information that Fortinbras *had* intended to invade Denmark, but that the King of Norway has now persuaded him to invade Poland instead. Will the Danes object to this crossing Danish territory with an army? No, the Danes have no objection, so Fortinbras makes another appearance, this time on his way to Poland with his army, and Shakespeare makes a gallant attempt to anchor him in the play as he had already anchored the Hecuba scene by contrasting Fortinbras' resolution with Hamlet's weakness. Nor is this all. At the precise moment when Hamlet has been stabbed with the poisoned foil, he and his army return, and, hearing him approach, Hamlet, who has been dying in a cloud of the most exquisite poetry, sits up to give him his vote for the succession to the throne.

This is absurd enough for anything, but we reach craziness when Fortinbras, without asking anyone's leave, announces that he proposes to annex Denmark anyway, and Horatio, forgetting all about his dead friend, hurriedly begs him to do it quickly before anyone can anticipate him—

Even while men's minds are wild, lest some mischance
On plots, and errors happen.[1]

This is the point in his work where Shakespeare's anxiety about the future becomes almost hysterical. He had written immediately before it two other plays, both dealing with the danger of internal dissension and revolution. We know that 'Hamlet' was produced at Oxford and Cambridge; I am inclined to share Sir Edmund Chambers' view that 'Troilus and Cressida' was produced there, and I feel sure that the gagging passages between Hamlet and Polonius refer to a similar occasion.

[1] *Ham.*, v. 1.

—You played once i' th' university, you say?
—I did enact Julius Caesar; I was killed i' the Capitol: Brutus killed me.
—It was a brute part of him to kill so capital a calf.[1]

I can make nothing of this unless I assume that Polonius was played by the fat comedian who also took the parts of Sir Toby and Falstaff—'the fatted calf'—and that he also played Caesar ('let me have men about me that are fat') to Burbage's Brutus at a university production.

You may notice, besides, how Rosencrantz and Guildenstern expatiate on the dangers attending 'the cease of majesty'[2] and how Laertes arrives on the scene accompanied by a mob howling 'Laertes shall be king! Laertes king!'[3] You may notice the prosaic solder with which the Fortinbras scenes are joined in, such as 'I think it be no other but e'en so' and 'this business is very well ended', and perhaps agree with me that the date of those passages is probably the winter of 1602–3 when the old Queen lay dying and Cecil was trying to prepare public opinion for the accession of a most unpopular and unpleasant foreign prince, who, like Fortinbras, had in his time sketched invasions on the English border. It may be too much to assume that behind the tendentiousness of 'Troilus and Cressida' and 'Hamlet' was a certain understanding between Cecil and Shakespeare, but it certainly seems strange that one of James' first public acts on reaching London was to appoint Shakespeare's company his personal players with the rank of Grooms of the Chamber.

Shakespeare is never a critical, consistent writer, as Jonson is, and nowhere was his consistency so sorely tested as in 'Hamlet', for his view of life seems to have been darkening even as he worked over it. In his early plays and poems the attitude to death was a simple contradiction in

[1] *Ham.*, III. 2.   [2] *Ham.*, III. 3.   [3] *Ham.*, IV. 5.

terms—'Death is the end of Death'—but from the moment Hamlet begins his meditation on Suicide—a subject which was afterwards never very far from Shakespeare's thought —we know that it has no vestige of connection with the play; that it has been spatchcocked into the scene where it stands; that it is not the ghost-ridden Hamlet who speaks of 'the undiscovered country from whose bourne no traveller returns' or the heir to the throne who has felt 'the insolence of office and the spurns that patient merit of the unworthy takes'; we know that this, like the sonnets, or Audley's speech before Poitiers, or Richard's in prison, is personal poetry, and that a shadow has come over Shakespeare's mind. The Play scene with its delightful air of parody; the high comedy of Polonius, give place to this and the graveyard scene for Armin and his zany in which for the first time we find Shakespeare indulging a passion for macabre humour. In the latter there is a horror of the charnel house, stifled until the present moment, which would yet frame the pathetic inscription on his grave.

It is futile to speculate on the precise occasion of this melancholia. It may have been a dangerous illness, and it is interesting that Dr. Caroline Spurgeon has noticed in 'Hamlet' the prevalence of images dealing with internal tumours;[1] but this, at the best, can be only guess-work. What we can do is put our finger on passage after passage which seems to echo the work of Montaigne; his altophobia in 'the cliff that beetles o'er his base',[2] his views on fashions in handwriting in 'I once did hold it as our Statists do a baseness to write fair';[3] his quotation of Quintilian in the Player's tears; Etienne de la Boetie's phrase on death— ' 'Tis coming or 'tis past but present never' in 'If it be now 'tis not to come, if it be not to come it will be now';[4] most of all perhaps in that terrible phrase which Shakespeare was

[1] Caroline Spurgeon, *Shakespeare's Imagery*. [2] *Ham.*, I. 4. [3] *Ham.*, V. 2.
[4] *Ham.*, V. 2.

later to versify in 'Lear' and 'Cymbeline'—'I believe that which Plato says to be true that man was made by the gods to sport and play withal.'

Atheism was no new thing in Elizabethan England. Ralegh, Chapman, Harriot, Marlowe and Kyd were probably all free-thinkers, but theirs was not the sort of disbelief which would have been likely to affect Shakespeare. Marlowe's atheism is that of the outlaw; it is anti-social rather than anti-religious, and Shakespeare was never anti-social. Montaigne was the first compendium of classical philosophy which Shakespeare could have read, and he was a rationalist who did not leave one shred of traditional belief in the mind of a sympathetic reader; nothing but that sense of the utter futility of human existence by which Hamlet is haunted.

At bottom rationalism and realism are aspects of the same frame of mind, and sooner or later, both are bound to come up against the supreme test of the irrationality of the universe. All classical civilisation is summed up in that line of Sophocles, 'Never to have lived were best', or Mme de Sevigne's thought that the best of all fates had been to die in her nurse's arms, or Housman's 'O it was well with me in days ere I was born'. No rationalism which fails to allow for a missing sense in humanity can escape it. For more than ten years Shakespeare had given himself to the view that the business of the artist was 'to hold as 'twere a mirror up to Nature', and he was at the age when a realist who thinks at all is bound to ask himself if reality itself be real. I see no reason to suppose that any personal disillusionment such as the infidelity of a second Dark Lady caused the change in him. On the contrary, I feel that any explanation of that sort is not adequate to explain the change, and, given his genius, I do not see how he could possibly have escaped a religious crisis; or how the marvels of the imaginative universe which he had created could have failed to throw him back on the thought of his own extinction.

'Even the powerful mind of Johnson was foiled by futurity,' Boswell tells us, and the Meditation on Suicide expresses the horror of that shuddering sensibility before 'the Great Doom's image'. It sets the key for Claudio's 'Ay, but to die, and go we know not where',[1] and the Gaoler's 'for look you, sir, you know not which way you shall go',[2] and it is the very dizziness of the realistic height from which Shakespeare views it which gives him the tendency towards suicide, that longing to plunge at once into the abyss, 'to rush into the secret house of Death' and 'encounter Darkness like a bride and hug her in my arms!' —a strange distorted memory of Chapman's great line on the marriage night—

Fear fills the chamber, darkness decks the bride.[3]

After 'Hamlet' the attitude to death is perceptibly different. Shakespeare is no longer satisfied with the contradiction in terms, which he uses only once, and then only as a subsidiary argument. There is the revulsion against what to the rationalist appears to be the end of all, and then (merely because if it *is* the end of all, life itself is meaningless and we can merely shrink from its murderous claws) he is driven back upon death as the only thing 'which shackles accident and bolts up change' and sings its praises. Again and again we hear this contradiction set forth, and grow accustomed, first to the spasm of revulsion, and then the constrained celebration of the only power which can quit us of the contradictions, the burnings and freezings—

Fear no more the heat o' the sun,
Nor the furious winter's rages[4]

[1] *M. for M.*, III. 1.   [2] *Cym.*, v. 4.   [3] *Hero and Leander*.   [4] *Cym.*, IV. 2

It is the presence of this new attitude to death which gives 'Hamlet' its dual nature. In Polonius the antithesis is still open; there is still 'I' and 'you', but in the shuddering sensibility of Hamlet's reproaches to his mother and the morbid humour of the graveyard scene the jaws of the antithesis begin to close, and we revert to the Shakespeare of 'Henry VI' and a drama which takes place only in the theatre of the poet's mind.

But what a difference there is in that mind!

IX

'OTHELLO' is the first play in which the excess of personal emotion which we notice in 'Hamlet' is allowed to swing the action, and in 'Lear' it rages like the storm. These two plays are among the greatest dramatic poems in the world; they are the work of a stage-hand whose skill is almost supernatural; yet they seem to me failures.

First of all, we must dismiss the idle speculation which finds in Othello's jealousy a key to Shakespeare's gloom. The flightiness of Cressida, the facility of Hamlet's mother, the doubts of Desdemona's virtue, do not mean that Shakespeare had met with another Dark Lady. They are part of a general abandonment of human values, aspects of a despair with human existence which can only be described as misanthropy.

The technical trouble with 'Othello' is that it is high tragedy based on the scenario of a comic opera. It is not improved by Shakespeare's treatment, for in his source he had plenty of motive for Iago's conduct, had he chosen to use it, but he did not, and left Iago, like Richard III, a mere inexplicable figure of evil. The handkerchief is a motif from court comedy; Portia's ring all over again, and quite insufficient to support the weight of the tragedy he builds on it. The scene in which Othello overlooks a meeting between Iago and Cassio and translates Cassio's gestures and laughter into a comment on his supposed affair with Desdemona is another and cruder example. In court comedy it is possible that it might pass muster as a bit of good-humoured extravagance, but the convention is farcical, not tragic. The curious staginess of these tragedies reminds us of Hardy's novels, and the purpose seems to be the same. Shakespeare puts the Almighty on trial for murder and then fakes the evidence. Now, it is the essence of high tragedy that the more demands the author makes on our emotions, the more he will concede to our intelligence; the higher he keys his tragedy and flings his sceptre at the injurious gods, the more he will need to convince us, as Sophocles and Racine do, that his statements are true and his conclusions inescapable, and that is the test 'Othello' will not stand up to. There is more of the inescapable feeling of high tragedy in the scene from 'Troilus and Cressida' in which Ulysses and Troilus overhear the lovemaking of Diomede and Cressida than in anything in 'Othello' up to the actual climax.

At the same time it would be foolish not to appreciate the way in which the abandonment of realism, the bursting of the dykes, releases a flood of passion and poetry. Undoubtedly, for years the poet in Shakespeare had been half-strangled by his theoretical realism; the filter of human beings through whom it had to pass before reaching the audience had let through only a trickle from the vast reservoir of his imagination. Now it tears out, inundating and fertilising great tracts of country. The moment the wretched machinery which precipitates the crisis has served its purpose, the play leaps on to a new plane.

One can see it best in the astonishing silences and half-silences of the text. There are the stunned repetitions. 'He echoes me as if there were some monster in his thought too hideous to be shown.'

> —Thy husband knew it all.
> —My husband.
> —Thy husband.
> —That she was false to wedlock?
> —Ay, with Cassio. . . .
> —My husband.

> —Ay, 'twas he that told me first:
>   An honest man he is, and hates the slime
>   That sticks on filthy deeds.
> —My husband![1]

Time and again it is as though the mind were so stunned that it could not respond, and then again it leaps out in blazing hypersensibility, too vivid to remain for long upon the level of conscious thought and diving back into itself again so that we are bewildered by its responses. 'And good lieutenant, I think you think I love you?' says Iago. 'I have well approved it, sir,' replies Cassio. 'I drunk!' And there is Othello's:

> —Sir, she can turn and turn, and yet go on,
>   And turn again; and she can weep, sir, weep;
>   And she's obedient as you say, obedient,
>   Very obedient. Proceed you in your tears.
>   Concerning this, sir—O well-painted passion!—
>   I am commanded home. Get you away;
>   I'll send for you anon. Sir, I obey. . . .[2]

But the fundamental weakness of the play is simply that it is not interesting. In tragedy we know what the end must be, but the dramatic interest is in the details of the fight between destiny and a character not unmatched with it; the way in which destiny is foiled and recovers; in which the original simple doom is thwarted. But in 'Othello' there is no fight, and there is no dramatic interest in watching through round after round the suffering of someone who cannot hit back, and Othello, Desdemona and Cassio are all passive figures, and the only active figure in the play is an abstraction. If Iago, after playing the trick of the handkerchief had realised the danger in which he had involved

[1] *Oth.*, V. 2.   [2] *Oth.*, IV. I.

himself by goading Othello too far; if then in terror he had set about trying to avert the inevitable catastrophe, we should have had drama and Othello would have ceased to be a passive figure, but I do not think that such a scenario would have satisfied Shakespeare at all. He was not interested in tragedy as such; he was interested only in saying what he had to say, and Iago, the puppet, was the only medium through which he could say it.

The same is true of 'King Lear'. Even as a child I always found it impossible to stomach the first scene in this play, and had the feeling, fatal to the appreciation of tragedy, 'the man's a fool'. A king divides his kingdom up among his three daughters, and then disinherits the favourite for refusing to join in a competition of flattery. Kent, the honest courtier who has defended her, is exiled. That opening scene would damn any play. But as it was part of his source-material we had better pass it and see what Shakespeare added to it. The king's follower, Gloucester, then disinherits and banishes his son, Edgar, on the unsupported allegations of his natural son, Edmund, and we are presented with a double plot involving two baneful and deluded old fathers, two sets of wicked children and two sets of dutiful ones. Kent returns to the king's service in disguise in time to see Lear's wicked children drive him from their homes, insane, while Gloucester's son, Edmund, conspires with them to murder his own father. Regan and her husband between them tear out the old man's eyes. The two dutiful children set about restoring the balance. Edgar, pretending to be a madman—'it may appear to some ridiculous'—to escape his father's vengeance, meets the old man with his eye-sockets still bleeding after his mutilation. He wants to commit suicide and asks Edgar to lead him to a certain high cliff. Instead, Edgar leads him to a hillock which he describes as a huge cliff, and the old man hurls himself off it, and is of course uninjured. Then Edgar comes up, this time in his proper person, and persuades his father that the hillock really had been a cliff, his guide a fiend trying to lure him to destruction, his escape a miracle. Then he goes out to challenge his wicked brother who, with his last dying kick, orders the hanging of Cordelia.

Now, seriously, what are we to make of this tissue of nonsense masquerading as tragedy? There is something dreadfully wrong with that particular scene between Edgar and his father. The playwright may show his hand too soon —the beginner's mistake—or too late—the journeyman's. If Shakespeare really was responsible for the scenario of 'Lear' he shows it too late. The moment is past when we can be moved by the meeting between the deluded father and his wronged son, and no tragic dramatist in his right mind would ever deliberately have sacrificed such a scene merely to extract another rabbit from the dramatic hat. There is a second example of a delayed climax at the end of 'Measure for Measure' which is even clumsier.

In presence of a crude collaborator we may, if we choose, bring in a verdict of 'not proven' regarding the blood-thirsty tomfoolery of Barnardine and Roggazine in 'Measure for Measure'; even perhaps the bringing in of Macbeth's head on a pole; but we cannot acquit Shakespeare of the same sort of tomfoolery over Cloten's body in 'Cymbeline' or the stamping out of Gloucester's eyes in 'Lear'. They are part of the psychological wantonness of which the later plays are full. When Shakespeare opened the dykes, something more than poetry came in. Cymbeline banishes Posthumus in a childish frenzy like Lear's, or Gloucester's; Posthumus, himself banished, in a childish frenzy like Othello's, believes some nonsense about Imogen's fidelity and orders her murder. 'A Winter's Tale' opens with a king who, for no particular reason, imagines that his wife has deceived him with Polixenes, and orders the murder of

Polixenes, the trial of his wife, and first the burning and then abandonment of his new-born baby Perdita. (In this welter of neuroticism it is merely a detail that the kind old courtier who is compelled to expose her is eaten by a bear—presumably Shakespeare's company *had* a bear.) Perdita in turn falls in love with Polixenes' son, whereupon Polixenes orders the execution of her supposed father and the banishment of everybody. And even stranger than the phantasmagoria of men mad with jealousy and power is the fantasy of girls with pretty-pretty names—Cordelia, Perdita, Miranda and Imogen; the passive principle opposed to the active one. There is no trace of the ambiguity which defines the characters of Richard II, Shylock or Falstaff. Nothing opposes the storm of misanthropy which blows through these later plays, and we can hardly escape the feeling that the image of the burst seed-pod which we find for the first time in 'Lear' and again in 'Macbeth', 'Timon of Athens' and 'A Winter's Tale', represents Shakespeare's own thought.

> Crack Nature's moulds, all germens spill at once
> That make ungrateful man.[1]

The misanthropy is, of course, common to other writers. European civilisation, as re-introduced by James I, had some features which must have appeared unfamiliar to Englishmen. Thanks to their virtual isolation during Elizabeth's long reign they were in some ways far ahead of their contemporaries on the Continent, but generally far behind. The Renaissance had influenced them deeply, but they were still mediaeval, almost Catholic in outlook; and this came out whenever they tried to express themselves in architecture, prose or drama. The Elizabethan theatre with its canopied stage, half a picture stage, half a platform set up

[1] *Lear*, III. 2.

in an innyard, is typically transitional in character; something which must change immediately. The typical Tudor building, full of memories of Gothic and rumours of the Renaissance, is merely a temporary compromise.

Elizabeth, as wise as James was foolish, realised that absolute monarchy in a country politically as mature as England was a risky business, and for a woman it might have been fatal. She steered a clever middle course, ruling as she said (not altogether insincerely) by her people's love. Middle-class opinion counted for a good deal. Shakespeare and his company were still what the middle classes considered them; rogues and vagabonds. One of James' first acts was to make them Grooms of the Chamber. 'Kings,' he explained, 'are not only God's lieutenants upon earth and sit upon God's throne, but even by God himself they are called gods.' Shakespeare versified it in 'Sir Thomas More'.

> (God) hath not only lent the King his figure,
> His throne and sword, but given him his own name,
> Calls him a god on earth.[1]

'I think the King is but a man as I am,' said the disguised Henry on the night before Agincourt, and here Shakespeare was expressing the humane and pitiful Elizabethan view of the monarch who, in Daniel's noble lines—

> Environed with deceit, hemmed in with guile,
> Soothed up in flattery, fawned on of all,
> Within his own living as in exile,
> Hears but with others' ears or not at all.[2]

Absolutism had come in and with it its characteristic art. 'Princes' images on their tombs do not lie as they were

---

[1] *Sir Thomas More*, II. 4.   [2] *Civil Wars*.

wont,' says Webster, 'seeming to pray up to Heaven, but with their hands under their cheeks, as if they died of the toothache.'[1] 'Othello' and 'Lear' are Baroque tragedies as 'Measure for Measure' and 'Cymbeline' are Baroque comedies. They have all the characteristic of Baroque art; the sensationalism, the extravagant emotional attitudes, 'as if they had died of the toothache'; the sentimentality, particularly in the portraits of women; even the desire to shock. Shakespeare leads the fashion rather than follows it, for the 'romances' do not begin with 'Philaster' or 'Pericles' but with 'Othello' and 'Lear'. Evade the physical catastrophe of 'Lear' and you have a Baroque comedy; add the final catastrophe to 'A Winter's Tale' and you have a Baroque tragedy.

But one cannot place the responsibility entirely on any form of art, however fashionable it may have been. That must rest on Shakespeare himself and the blind tyrannous strength which would not be satisfied with anything but inhuman abstractions like Iago and Edmund as the instruments of destiny, and which uses them in an overmastering impulse to crush and destroy, even to the very seed in the womb.

[1] *The Duchess of Malfi*, IV. 2.

X

THE commentators suggest that there is a lightening of
the misanthropic gloom in 'Macbeth' and 'Antony and
Cleopatra', but this is merely the rounding-off of a senti-
mental romance composed by themselves of which the hero
is not Shakespeare but Beethoven. These two plays are
outstanding among the tragedies not because Shakespeare
was becoming optimistic but because they are histories, and
his job being mainly one of interpretation, he could not
wreak his misanthropy on them.

In them the nervous disintegration of language which
was hinted at in earlier plays becomes marked. 'Hamlet'
and 'Troilus and Cressida', apart from their classicisms and
gallicisms, contain a number of grammatical perversions;
nouns are used as verbs, adjectives as nouns and so forth.
'To business' from 'Hamlet' is typical, and I fancy that
when the writer or printer punctuated the lines 'No, let the
candied tongue, lick absurd pomp and crook the pregnant
hinges of the knee',[1] he meant precisely that and not the
mixed metaphor of 'No, let the candied tongue lick absurd
pomp' to which modern editors correct it. In 'Lear' we get
rather more of it: verbs like 'stranger', 'monster', 'worthy',
'hovel' and 'knee', and adjectives like 'looped', 'windowed'
and 'husbanded'. In 'Antony and Cleopatra' it becomes a
landslide; coined verbs like 'ballad', 'boy', 'antick',
'spaniel', 'lackey', 'boot', 'bark', 'safe' and 'demure', as
well as the even more characteristic nouns in 'er' like
'sworder', 'master-leaver', 'hater', 'equaliser', 'feeder' and
'homager', particularly in harsh compounds like 'putter-
out'. Transitive verbs tend to become intransitive and the

[1] *Ham.*, III. 2.

other way round, while on the analogy of 'honour' ('the honours were equal') abstract nouns are given plurals as in 'shames' and 'decays'.

In metre there is an even greater disintegration, the midline stop of 'Hamlet' giving place to a full close in the middle of a line, sometimes produced by a harsh combination of assonance and alliteration, sometimes by a powerful heaping up of qualified nouns.

> Her brother's ghost his paved bed would break
> And take her hence in horror.[1]

In 'Antony and Cleopatra' there is even a looseness of metre which suggests the metrical experiments of Jonson and Fletcher with their abuse of the feminine ending. The trouble with this is that by infection the feminine ending spreads to the middle of the line, and when the two move together, as they frequently do in Fletcher, the five-beat measure of blank verse breaks down and we get one of four beats which is quite unsuitable to drama. Shakespeare's ear was too sensitive to make this mistake often but he makes it in 'Cymbeline' and 'Antony and Cleopatra'.

> —And I' have heard' Apol'lodorus ca'rried—
> —No more' of that'; he did' so.
> —   What, I pray' you?
> —A cer'tain queen' to Cae'sar on a mat'tress.[2]

It seems to me that it is in a group of plays which I conjecture to have been written about 1605—'Macbeth', certain scenes from 'Measure for Measure' and odd speeches in that strange medley of authors and styles 'All's Well That Ends Well' that Shakespeare's style reached perfection. Experiment in these has gone as far as it could go without

[1] *M. for M.*, v. 1.   [2] *A. & C.*, ii. 6.

injuring the texture of the verse. In 'Macbeth' particularly, the peculiar mood of exaltation is expressed in the fondness for the word 'great' used for colour rather than sense: 'the great Doom's image'; 'in the great hand of God'; 'our great quell'. The exaltation checks the misanthropy which emerges only occasionally as in the repetition of the theme of the broken seed-pod in 'Lear'—

> though the treasure
> Of Nature's germens tumble all together
> Even till Destruction sicken.[1]

But the misanthropy appears principally in the fact that the play is less a tragedy of crime than of ambition; that Macbeth is less a good man who has done wrong than an ambitious one who has discovered the mockery of power. There is a markedly subjective note in this. Death, the ultimate horror, he has inflicted on Duncan, but Duncan in his grave has the peace which Macbeth has not; 'steel nor poison, malice domestic, foreign levy, nothing, can touch him further.[2] 'Fear no more the frown of the great, thou art past the tyrant's stroke.'[3]

Unfortunately, 'Macbeth' is one of a group of plays which raise problems that have never been solved. It is not in its entirety the play which Simon Forman saw at the Globe in 1610, for the witch scenes in this were treated differently, and there was a scene, now lost, in which Macbeth and his wife unsuccessfully tried to wash the blood from their hands—the scene which is echoed in the Sleepwalking Scene. Editors are generally agreed that the text has been cut and additions made to it. It is very corrupt, and Shakespeare can hardly be accused of writing cacophonous nonsense like:

---

[1] *Macb.*, IV. 1.   [2] *Macb.*, III. 2.   [3] *Cym.*, IV. 2.

> *if* th' assassination
> Could trammel up the consequence and catch
> With his surcease, success: *that but* this blow
> Might *be* the *be*-all and the end-all. *Here*
> *But here* upon this bank and shoal of time
> We'd jump the life to come. *But* in these cases
> We still have judgment *here, that* we *but* teach etc.[1]

Sir Edmund Chambers would confine the non-Shakespearean passages to the scenes involving Hecate; others would go further and banish the witches altogether. It is generally assumed that the cuts and additions were made after Shakespeare left the theatre, and on the strength of the title of a song which is found in full in Middleton's 'Witch' the additions have been ascribed to him. I think the editors are on the wrong tack here. Forman, who summarises very carefully what he saw, makes no mention of the apparition scene which could scarcely have escaped his attention, and the apparition scene is undoubtedly Shakespeare's, and the parts of the witches are closely integrated with it.

But it seems to me that the editors have ignored the most obvious signs of what they call 'revision'. One scene opens like this:

Lady M.   Is Banquo gone from court?
Serv.   Ay, madam, but returns again tonight.
Lady M.   Say to the King I would attend his leisure
        For a few words.
Serv.   Madam, I will.   (*Exit* Servant.)
Lady M.   Nought's had all's spent
        Where our desire is got without content:
        'Tis safer to be that which we destroy
        Than by destruction dwell in doubtful joy.
                    (*Enter* Macbeth.)[2]

[1] *Macb.*, I. 7.   [2] *Macb.*, III. 2.

Now there are two remarkable things about this passage. The first is the extraordinary clumsiness of the preparation for Macbeth's entry; the Servant has been introduced merely to summon him, while the couplets are a mere stop-gap between his departure and Macbeth's entrance. The second is that the couplets recur in a vastly superior blank verse form in Macbeth's first speech after his entrance.

> Better be with the dead
> Whom we to gain our peace have sent to peace
> Than on the torture of the mind to lie
> In restless ecstasy.[1]

At first sight it would appear as if the 'reviser' had translated Shakespeare's blank verse into rhymed couplets to fill a gap in a scene of his own. But is this what did happen? 'All's Well That Ends Well', at least so far as the verse goes, must be almost contemporary with 'Macbeth'. There is a similar use of the word 'great' for colour rather than sense: 'our great self', 'the great Compt' and 'the great sender'. It is a play about a poor girl who, having got herself married to a nobleman, tricks him into consummating the marriage by acting as substitute for an Italian girl he is courting. As in 'Macbeth' there is a lot of dreary rhymed verse, but the peculiar feature of this is that it is Shakespeare who translates the rhymed couplets into blank verse, by a few strokes transforming them into magnificent poetry. Take this, for instance.

> But O strange men!
> That can such sweet use make of what they hate
> When saucy trusting of the cozened thoughts
> Defiles the pitchy night: *so lust doth play*
> *With what it loathes for that which is away.*[2]

[1] *Macb.*, III. 2.   [2] *A.W.E.W.*, IV. 4.

Or this, with its characteristic repetition of the 'Ne'er loved till lost' theme which haunted him:

> Love that comes too late
> Like a remorseful pardon slowly carried
> To the great sender turns a sour offence
> Crying 'That's good that's gone.' Our rash faults
> *Make trivial price of serious things we have*
> *Not knowing them until we know their grave*:
> *Oft our displeasures to ourselves unjust*
> *Destroy our friends and after weep their dust, etc.*[1]

As Professor Wilson has pointed out, we can actually see the rhymes through the blank verse (I had noticed this before seeing the New Cambridge Edition, and my collection of rhymes is rather larger).

> Religious in my error, I *adore*
> The sun that looks upon his worshipper
> But knows of him no *more*.[2]

Or (an even more striking example):

> . . . that cans't not *dream*
> We poising us in her defective scale,
> Can weigh thee to the *beam*; that wilt not *know*
> It is in us to plant thine honour where
> We please to have it *grow*.[3]

The scene from which the latter passage is taken is an extraordinary bit of work. It opens with Bertram, Lafeu and Parolles discussing Helena's restoration of the King to health, though Bertram's sole contribution to the discussion

[1] *A.W.E.W.*, v. 3.   [2] *A.W.E.W.*, i. 3.   [3] *A.W.E.W.*, ii. 3.

is the interjection 'And so 'tis.' Then the King and Helena appear, accompanied by courtiers and taking no notice of Lafeu and Parolles, while Bertram, without any leave-taking, is presently discovered among the wards whom the King summons in order that Helena may choose herself a husband. When she has done this, Lafeu and Parolles 'stay behind, commenting of this wedding' as a curious stage direction informs us. I am confident that Bertram's presence at the opening of the scene is a mistake and that his real entrance is with the other wards; and that the scene in verse has been unskilfully thrust into a prose duet between Lafeu and Parolles, or rather that the prose duet has been built about the scene in verse. Furthermore I feel sure that the author of the prose scene must be the same man who worked over the verse and has given an occasional remark to Lafeu in order to link him somehow with the action. Take, for instance, the lines in which Helena chooses her husband.

King. ... Fair maid, send forth thine eye: this youthful parcel
　　　　Of noble bachelors stand at my bestowing,
　　　　O'er whom both sovereign power and father's voice
　　　　I have to *use*: thy frank election *make*;
　　　　Thou hast power to *choose* and they none to *forsake*.
Hel. 　To each of you one fair and virtuous mistress
　　　　Fall when love please! marry, to each but one!
Laf. 　I'd give bay Curtal and his furniture
　　　　My mouth were no more broken than these boys'
　　　　And writ as little beard.
King. 　　　　　　　　　　　Peruse them well
　　　　Not one of those but had a noble father.
Hel. 　Gentlemen,
　　　　Heaven hath through me restored the king to *health*.
All. 　We understand it and thank Heaven for you.

Hel.   I am a simple maid and therein *wealthiest*
That I protest I simply am a maid.
Please it your majesty, I have done already:
The blushes in my cheeks thus whisper me,
'We blush that thou should'st *choose*; but be *refused*
Let the white death sit on thy cheek forever;
We'll ne'er come there again.'
King.   Make choice; and *see*,
Who shuns thy love shuns all his love in *me*.[1]

Now who can doubt that this is a scene in rhymed verse which has been lightly revised, or doubt that the reviser was Shakespeare? It contains some of his most thrilling verse, but the couplets stick up through it, not only in obvious rhymes like 'health-wealthiest', 'choose-use', 'choose-refused', but also in the suppressed rhymes of 'parcel ('band')-stand' and 'election ('voice')-choice'.

This is not the only evidence for a second hand because at the end of the verse scene we get the note that 'Parolles and Lafeu stay behind commenting of this wedding', which, as Professor Wilson points out, is not a stage direction at all and can only be explained as an instruction to a collaborator. He takes the view that it is Shakespeare who gives the order; I believe it is the scenarist who drafted the original scene in rhymed couplets which Shakespeare worked over, and that Shakespeare wrote the prose scenes at either side of it. The 'dictionary line' given to Lafeu and Pavolles in the latter 'In a most weak and debile minister' is very like Shakespeare's hand.

It might well be, of course, that Shakespeare sometimes found it more convenient to draft his scenes in rhymed couplets, nor with 'Timon of Athens' in mind do I think we should entirely dismiss that possibility; but there is

[1] *A.W.E.W.*, II. 3.

evidence that this is not what happened with 'All's Well That Ends Well'. The scene continues:

Hel.   Now, Dian, from thy altar do I fly,
       And to imperial Love, that god most high,
       Do my sighs stream. Sir, will you hear my suit?
1st L. And grant it.
Hel.   Thanks, sir; all the rest is mute.
Laf.   I had rather be in this choice than throw ames ace
       for my life.
Hel.   The honour, sir, that flames in your fair eyes,
       Before I speak, too threateningly replies:
       Love make your fortune twenty times above
       Her that so wishes and her humble love.
2nd L. No better, if you please.
Hel   My wish receive,
       Which great Love grant! and so I take my leave.
Laf.   Do all they deny her? An they were sons of mine,
       I'd have them whipped; or I would send them to
       the Turk to make eunuchs of.
Hel.   Be not afraid that I your hand should take;
       I'll never do you wrong for your own sake:
       Blessings upon your vows, and in your bed
       Find fairer fortune if you ever wed.
Laf.   These boys are boys of ice, they'll none have her:
       sure they are bastards to the English; the French
       ne'er got 'em.[1]

Now, as Professor Wilson points out, the meaning of this is that all the lads except Bertram are eager to be selected, and Helena, like the great lady she is, lets them down lightly by affecting to believe that they are really alarmed at the prospect. The curious thing is that this is what Lafeu believes also. Professor Wilson puts him and Parolles

[1] *A.W.E.W.*, II. 3.

'at a distance', but I cannot imagine any stage distance sufficient to make this point clear to an audience. Just think of the difficulties that face a producer. He must make it plain that the young lords are eager to be chosen as Helena's partner though none of them has a line which makes this sufficiently clear; that Helena is determined on having none of them while expressing her belief that none of them will have her, and that Lafeu who completely misinterprets the whole scene is merely making a mistake. Without testing it in rehearsal, I should say the result would be wholesale confusion. Surely, what has happened is that in his careless reading of the scene which he has been partially revising, Shakespeare has made precisely the mistake which Professor Wilson accuses Lafeu of making, and assumed that the young men have no desire to marry Helena. After all, it is a very natural mistake, for the lines are so indecisive that they may be interpreted either way.

It is not until we reach 'Measure for Measure' that we really get sufficient material for literary criticism. The New Cambridge editor, Professor Wilson, has produced a most brilliant analysis of the text, but the conclusions he draws are disappointing. They are that the play was abridged for Court performance on December 26th, 1604, and, some time after November, 1606, expanded again in prose, Shakespeare not being consulted in either operation. He credits Shakespeare with 1865 lines; 'of these 1604 are in blank verse, and no one we think will be inclined to doubt that all this, whether its style be early or late, is from Shakespeare's hand.'[1] The rest of the play is the 'reviser's'.

The story is roughly that the Duke of Vienna retires to a monastery, leaving the government of the city in the hands of the puritanical Angelo, who re-enacts the laws against fornication, and condemns Claudio to death. Claudio's sister, Isabella, a novice in a convent, pleads for him, and

[1] *M. for M.* (New Cambridge Shakespeare).

Angelo offers to reprieve him if she becomes his mistress. The Duke, now acting as chaplain to the prison, overhears her telling this to her brother, and persuades her to allow a lady jilted by Angelo, one 'Mariana of the Moated Grange', to keep the tryst instead of her. Angelo, believing that he has possessed Isabella, and afraid of her brother's vengeance, sends a warrant for his head. The Duke has the head of another prisoner sent him instead, and then stages a finale in which Isabella accuses Angelo who gives her the lie; Mariana refutes Isabella, claiming Angelo for herself and in her turn is repudiated (all, scene for scene very much in the manner of 'All's Well That Ends Well') until finally the Duke himself slips off, and returning again in his monk's habit, makes a fresh accusation before revealing his identity, resurrecting Claudio and proposing to Isabella.

There is nothing whatever wrong with the main theme. It might have made a magnificent tragedy in the manner of 'Othello'; a fine study of a weak man in the manner of 'Promos and Cassandra', or a satiric comedy like 'Tartufe'. All these possibilities were barred, because on to the original powerful tale has been grafted the fanciful theme of 'All's Well That Ends Well', and the introduction of 'Mariana of the Moated Grange' at once makes it necessary that Angelo shall be pardoned and robs the play of all dramatic impulse.

How did Shakespeare come to write such a play? I suggest that he wrote it on a scenario prepared by the same man who prepared the scenario of 'All's Well That Ends Well' and that most of the play as we have it is the collaborator's work. The evidence for this is of a different kind from that in 'All's Well That Ends Well'. There are rhymed couplets in 'Measure for Measure' and some are manifestly not Shakespeare's, but there is far more impressive evidence than this. In iii. 1 there is a change from verse to prose of which the New Cambridge editors write with commendable restraint that 'the two halves of this scene cannot be made of a piece by anyone possessing even a rudimentary acquaintance with English prose and poetry. We will not say they could not have been written—an interval granted—by the same man. But we say confidently that they could not have been written by the same man at one spell, on one inspiration, or with anything like an identical or even continuous poetic purpose.'[1] Even this mild claim is rejected by the editor of the Temple Shakespeare who tells us that 'Shakespeare wrote the scene with a deliberately *dis*continuous *dramatic* purpose'—whatever that may be![2]

Shakespeare did not write the scene at all, at any time, and the evidence is not the difference in style—though Heaven knows that is obvious enough for anyone; it is in two passages which I must quote in full. The act opens in the prison with the Duke (disguised as a friar), Claudio *and the Provost*. (We shall see later what the significance of the Provost is.) The Duke comforts Claudio in the great speech on death and then Isabella's voice is heard outside.

Isab. What ho! Peace here; grace and good company!
Prov. Who's there? come in: the wish deserves a welcome.
Duke. Dear sir, ere long I'll visit you again.
Claud. Most holy sir, I thank you. (*Enter* Isabella.)
Isab. My business is a word or two with Claudio.
Prov. And very welcome. Look signior, here's your sister.
Duke. Provost, a word with you.
Prov. As many as you please.
Duke. Bring me to hear them speak where I may be concealed.   (*Exeunt* Duke *and* Provost.)[3]

[1] *M. for M.* (New Cambridge Shakespeare).   [2] *M. for M.* (Temple Shakespeare).   [3] *M. for M.*, III. I.

Now, this is a remarkable passage in itself, a fussy, confused and undramatic passage, but nothing like one which occurs a little later. In one of the greatest scenes in all literature Isabella tells her brother of Angelo's proposal; he breaks down and begs her to accept it, and she scorns him. Her speech is interrupted by the sudden emergence of the Duke from hiding, and it is of this joint that the New Cambridge editors say that 'the two halves of this scene cannot be made of a piece by anyone possessing even a rudimentary acquaintance with English prose and poetry'. It is curious that they fail to notice that the style of the second part is identical with that of the brief passage I have just quoted.

Duke.   Vouchsafe a word, young sister, but one word.

Isab.   What is your will?

Duke   Might you dispense with your leisure, I would by and by have some speech with you: *the satisfaction I would require is likewise your own benefit,*

Isab.   I have no superfluous leisure; my stay must be stolen out of other affairs; but I will attend you awhile. (*Walks apart.*)

Duke.   Son, I have overheard what hath passed between you and your sister. Angelo had never the purpose to corrupt her; only he hath made an assay of her virtue to practice his judgment with the disposition of natures; she, having the truth of honour in her, hath made him that gracious denial which he is most glad to receive. I am confessor to Angelo, and I know this to be true; therefore prepare yourself to death; do not satisfy your resolution with hopes that are fallible; tomorrow you must die; go to your knees and make ready.

Claud.   Let me ask my sister pardon. I am so out of love with life that I will sue to be rid of it.

Duke.	Hold you there: farewell. (*Exit* Claudio.)
	Provost, a word with you! (*Re-enter* Provost.)
Prov.	What's your will, father?
Duke.	That now you are come you will be gone. Leave me awhile with the maid: my mind promises with my habit no loss shall touch her by my company.
Prov.	In good time.[1]

The curious points of this passage are numerous; first, the phrase I have italicised and to which I shall return; secondly, the revelation of the secrets of the confessional which I am perhaps unreasonable in supposing that a friend of Southampton might have known more about; thirdly, the deliberate and cruel lying of the Duke; fourthly, the fact that Claudio, having asked leave to beg his sister's pardon, goes out without saying a word to her (where? the stage manager in me insists on asking). But all these become unimportant beside the one glaring fact that the author has not the remotest idea of how to get people on or off the stage. He has had to get Isabella to 'walk aside' while lies are told to her brother; he has had to get the prisoner out of the condemned cell unaccompanied by any gaoler to allow the Duke to talk to Isabella; worst of all he has had to withdraw the Provost from his hiding-place and dismiss him. This is beyond question the writing of a man who did not know the theatre.

But why has he tied himself up into this extraordinary knot? The explanation is perfectly simple. Neither the Duke nor the Provost has any business on the stage at all. In Shakespeare's version of the scene Claudio and Isabella must have fought out their battle to a conclusion, whatever it was. You can now see why I italicised the presence of Provost at the opening of the scene. He must be there to put the Duke in hiding, and when the Duke leaves his

[1] *M. for M.*, III. I.

hiding-place, and Claudio, whom he is supposed to be guarding, has wandered out of the cell unaccompanied, he must be summoned and dismissed in the most ridiculous lines of dramatic literature. 'What's your will, father?— That now you are come you will be gone.' Here one can go considerably further than the New Cambridge editors and say that no one possessing a rudimentary acquaintance with playwriting can possibly suppose this is the work of a dramatist.

But if not, what is he? Professor Wilson believes he is the man who revised and expanded the play at some time after November, 1606, but in this scene we have positive proof that he was not expanding but telescoping, in the manner of the man who telescoped two different scenes in 'The Two Gentlemen of Verona'. Let us see if we cannot find other traces of his hand.

In the opening scene of the fourth act which editors love to place at 'the Moated Grange at St. Luke's' a boy sings the heavenly 'Take O take those lips away' and is dismissed as the Duke enters to a volley of rhymed couplets.

Mar.   Let me excuse me, and believe me so,
       My mirth it much displeased, but pleased my woe.
Duke. 'Tis good; though music oft hath such a charm
       To make bad good, and good provoke to harm.
       I pray you, tell me, hath any body inquired for me here to-day? much upon this time have I promised here to meet.
Mar.   You have not been inquired after: I have sat here all day.   (*Enter* Isabella.)
Duke. I do constantly believe you. The time is come even now. I shall crave your forbearance a little: may be I will call upon you anon, *for some advantage to yourself.*

Mar.   I am always bound to you.   (*Exit* Mariana.).[1]

Mariana's exit at this point is the low-water-mark of dramatic incompetence, but surely we have met before this man who finds such inordinate difficulty in exits and entrances, and who tries to cover up the hugger-mugger in which he involves himself by making his characters say mysteriously '*It shall be for your good.*' Here he comes again, now that Isabella has explained the details of her arrangement for meeting Angelo.

Duke. [1]'Tis well borne up.
          I have not yet made known to Mariana
          A word of this. What ho! within! come forth!
                        (*Re-enter* Mariana.)
          I pray you, be acquainted with this maid;
          She comes to do you good.
Isab.   I do desire the like.
Duke. Do you persuade yourself that I respect you?
Mar.   Good friar, I know you do, and have found it.
Duke. Take then, this your companion by the hand,
          Who hath a story ready for your ear.
          I shall attend your leisure: but make haste;
          The vaporous night approaches.
Mar.   Will't please you walk aside?
                  (*Exeunt* Mariana *and* Isabella.)
Duke. O place and greatness! millions of false eyes
          Are stuck upon thee; volumes of report
          Run with these false and most contrarious quests
          Upon thy doings: thousand scapes of wit
          Make thee the father of their idle dreams
          And rack thee in their fancies.
                (*Re-enter* Mariana *and* Isabella.)
                  Welcome! How agreed?

[1] *M. for M.*, IV. I.

Isab. She'll take the enterprise upon her, father,
       If you advise it.[1]

Now every Shakespearean student has noticed one thing
about this scene: that the speech on 'Place and Greatness'
does not belong: clearly it belongs in iii. 2 where Lucio
traduces the Duke to the supposed Friar and the Duke says:

> No might nor greatness in mortality
> Can censure scape; back-wounding calumny
> The whitest virtue strikes. What king so strong
> Can tie the gall up in the slanderous tongue?[2]

Professor Wilson believes that the two passages are continuous and have been chopped up in this way because the
'reviser' wished to cover up a cut. Sir E. K. Chambers
believes they are not, and I feel sure he is right. We have
met before with precisely the same thing in 'Macbeth' only
that in 'Macbeth' the 'reviser' used his own couplets to
plug a hole, while here he is using Shakespeare's blank
verse. Why? To cover up a cut, replies Professor
Wilson. But is it? Surely, it is obvious that this is our old
friend who comes to do us good and finds such difficulty
about getting in and out to do it, and the reason he has used
Shakespeare's lines as a stop-gap is that by giving 'Mariana
of the Moated Grange' such a very awkward exit he has
tied himself into one of his usual knots. We must remember
that we are seeing Mariana for the first time; that she is
seeing Isabella for the first time, and that some sort
of exposition scene is necessary. The time for this is
immediately after Isabella's entrance: having failed to do
it then, the collaborator is faced with the necessity for
allowing either the Duke or Isabella to explain it all over
again to Mariana; and as his skill will not rise to this, he

[1] *M. for M.*, IV. I.   [2] *M. for M.*, III. 2.

cuts the Gordian knot by letting his ladies 'walk apart' while he uses six lines of Shakespeare quite irrelevantly to fill up the interval in which Isabella may be supposed to tell the story of her life to the other woman.

Once more, we can put our finger on this scene and say that it must be obvious to anyone with the remotest acquaintance with play-writing that it was not written by a dramatist. And wherever we look in the latter half of 'Measure for Measure' we come on the work of a man who was no dramatist. Another example occurs in the last act. The final rabbit is to be released from the hat; Claudio is to be produced safe and sound, so the Duke summons Barnardine who was to have been executed with him. There is a simple rule for summoning people on to the stage. They must either be on the stage or else they must be summoned before they are actually required. On no account must we have the impression that, like Lady Macbeth or the Duke, we are being made to 'attend their leisure'. The first scene of this very play shows how a dramatist does it.

Duke. I say, bid come before us Angelo.
                                        (*Exit* Attendant.)
          What figure, think you, of us he will bear? etc. etc.
                                        (*Enter* Angelo.)[1]

The last act yields a perfect example of how a dramatist does *not* do it.

Duke. . . . Go fetch him hither; let me look upon him.
                                        (*Exit* Provost.)
Escal. I am sorry, one so learned and so wise
          As you, Lord Angelo, have still appeared,

[1] *M. for M.*, I. I.

121

Should slip so grossly, both in the heat of blood
And lack of tempered judgement afterward.

Ang.   I am sorry that such sorrow I procure:

And so deep sticks it in my penitent heart
That I crave death more willingly than mercy;
'Tis my deserving, and I do entreat it.[1]

By this time we recognise our collaborator's little weakness, and glancing back we light upon the scene of Angelo's exposure to which this passage obviously belongs, and, turning the page, we find 'I have confessed her and I know her virtue' with (a few lines later) the final exit prepared by the inevitable 'I have a motion much imports your good'. It is only natural after the imaginative energy our benevolent collaborator has wasted in getting Claudio on to the stage that he should be too exhausted to give him even one line by which the audience might identify him. He had done the same thing in the prison scene. Searching further, we notice the hopelessly muffed second entrance of Isabella during the absence of the Duke.

Now, we definitely have a number of clues to the capacity of our collaborator, and can test other scenes for his presence. What, for instance, shall we make of this one? It is just before Angelo sends the order for Claudio's execution.

Duke.   The best and wholesomest spirits of the night

Envelop you, good Provost! Who called here of late?

Prov.   None since the curfew rung.
Duke.   Not Isabel?
Prov.   No.
Duke.   They will then ere't be long.
Prov.   What comfort is for Claudio?

[1] *M. for M.*, v. i.

Duke.   There's some in hope.
Prov.   It is a bitter deputy.
Duke.   Not so, not so; his life is paralleled
        Even with the stroke and line of his great justice:
        He doth with holy abstinence subdue
        That in himself which he spurs on his power
        To qualify in others: were he mealed with that
        Which he corrects, then were he tyrannous;
        But this being so he's just.   (*Knocking within.*)
                            Now are they come.
        (*aside*) This is a gentle provost: seldom when
        The steeled gaoler is the friend of men.
                            (*Knocking within.*)
        How now! What noise? That spirit's possessed
        with haste
        That wounds the unsisting postern with these
        strokes.
Prov.   There he must stay until the officer
        Arise to let him in: he is called up.
Duke.   Have you no countermand for Claudio yet?
                                    etc. etc.[1]

Here once more we have an entrance handled with child-
like incompetence. It is made still more incompetent by
editors who give the Provost an exit and immediate re-
entrance when the knocking is heard. As in the scene at
'The Moated Grange' we have the Duke calling to ask
whether someone hasn't enquired for him and when told
that no one has, giving the assurance that somebody soon
will. Again, we have a speech 'his life is paralleled' of pure
Shakespearean texture in a context where it is dramatically
meaningless, since the Duke already knows that Angelo's
'holy abstinence' does not exist; and once more we can
say confidently that this speech has been taken from its real

[1] *M. for M.*, IV. 2.

context which was probably a scene between the Duke and Lucio in which for the first time the Duke was told of Angelo's backsliding (the scene which in the revised play has been telescoped by the intrusion of the Duke and Provost into the prison scene), placed here with grotesque clumsiness to lengthen the interval between two successive entrances. If any reader has followed me so far, he will probably agree either that Shakespeare was writing 'with a deliberately *dis*continuous *dramatic* purpose' or that Professor Wilson's view that 'no one . . . will be inclined to doubt that all this, whether its style be early or late, is from Shakespeare's hand' is optimistic.

As with 'Macbeth' and 'All's Well That Ends Well' it seems quite clear that this is not a matter of revision but of collaboration. The two authors, probably working at a distance from one another, follow more or less the same scenario but have quite different approaches to the subject. Shakespeare's is grave and passionate as we can see from the frequency with which he repeats the name of God, though this is partly obscured by the editors' perpetuation of the meaningless Jacobean 'Heaven' in its place—

> Which sorrow is always towards ourselves, not *God*
> Showing we would not spare *God* as we love *Him*
> But as we stand in fear.[1]

The collaborator sees only a ballet of monks and nuns in the manner of 'The Merry Devil of Edmonton', though with nothing like the wit and grace of that little neglected masterpiece of the theatre; his is a slightly salacious and exceedingly sacreligious masquerade in which the disguised Duke hears everybody's confession and repeats the substance of it; and the characters enter to cheerful bursts of 'What ho! Peace ho!' It is notable that the opening of the

[1] *M. for M.*, II. 3.

scene between Isabella and Lucio in the convent of 'the Votarists of St. Clare' is in his style, which is marked by the use of un-Shakespearean words like 'manifested', 'affianced' and 'unsisting' (whatever that may be), and an extraordinarily stiff use of common words like 'constantly' and 'combine': 'I do *constantly* believe you'; 'I am *combined* by a sacred vow' and '*combinate* husband'.

So long as the scenario follows the original one of 'Promos and Cassandra' there is little fundamental disagreement between the collaborators. The first part of the play is masterly. But the collaborator was obsessed by the theme of 'All's Well That Ends Well' and failed to see that the introduction of 'Mariana of the Moated Grange' would inevitably result in a reconciliation scene which would call off the dogs of drama; and from the moment the lady's name is mentioned the collaboration begins to go to pieces. All the prose of the prison scene, in which we are told her past history, is the collaborator's; the scene at 'the Moated Grange' is entirely his idea. Shakespeare has conceived the play as one dealing with Angelo and Isabella; the collaborator as one about the Duke and Mariana; and again, it is notable that Shakespeare's Angelo never seems to have heard of the lady. As Professor Wilson points out of the collaborator in 'All's Well That Ends Well', the last word was his, and, as in 'Macbeth', the text of Shakespeare's portion is crudely cut and carelessly transcribed. 'If not a fedary but only he owe and succeed *thy* weakness'[1] is an obvious solecism, since not only does Isabella not know of Angelo's weakness, but she is speaking in the formal second person plural, and only breaks into the singular when she understands the full force of his proposal.

I do not pretend that this explanation covers all the difficulties though it covers most of them. It does not cover an impression of my own that the glorious scene of Pompey's

[1] *M. for M.*, II. 4.

examination before the magistrates is really early Shakespeare, written not for Armin but Kempe. The urbanity and detachment of Escalus' advice to Elbow—'because he hath some offences in him that thou wouldst discover if thou could'st, let him continue in his courses till thou knowest what they are'—has all the sunny quality of the Falstaff period. There is very little unadulterated Shakespeare in the later scenes, but what there is gives us an Elbow and a Pompey altered beyond recognition. It is not only that Shakespeare appears to be writing for different actors, but that he is writing out of a different conception of life. The poor Duke's constable has developed the sadistic snarl of the Baroque plays, and even Shakespeare fails to convince us that it is our old friend, Elbow, *alias* Dull, *alias* Verges, who says 'His neck will come to your waist— a cord, sir!'[1] This is the husky sniffle of the Gaoler in 'Cymbeline' with his 'O the charity of a penny cord!' the whine of the Pandar in 'Pericles' with his 'The poor Transylvanian is dead that lay with the little baggage.'[2] Sex and death; Pompey and Abhorson; this is the only sort of realism which the later Shakespeare permits himself.

There remains the question who the collaborator was, and here we can only fall back on speculation. I have an impression that the same man worked on 'The Merry Wives of Windsor', 'Macbeth', 'All's Well That Ends Well' and 'Pericles', and a suspicion which is little more than a fancy that he also had something to do with the scenarios of 'King Lear' and 'Cymbeline'. There is not sufficient of his work in any of these to identify him beyond doubt, and similarities of vocabulary such as 'manifested', which occurs only in the suspect portion of 'Merry Wives' and 'Measure for Measure', and 'vaporous', which occurs only in the Hecate scene of 'Macbeth' and in the Moated Grange scene of 'Measure for Measure', are slender. On the other

[1] *M. for M.*, III. 2.   [2] *Per.*, IV. 2.

hand, though it may be only a coincidence that the first dreary portion of 'Pericles' contains a few magnificent lines which everyone recognises as Shakespeare's, 'the blind mole casts copped hills towards heaven, to tell the earth is thronged by man's oppression,'[1] interpolated with no regard for their sense, I feel it can scarcely be an accident that again we get these cheerful explosions of 'Joy and all comfort in your sacred breast!' 'Peace to the lords of Tyre!' and 'Peace be at your labours!' or that the exit of an obviously Shakespearean scene should be prepared with 'If thou dost hear me it shall be for thy good.'[2] By an extraordinary coincidence we actually have external evidence that Shakespeare did not write 'it shall be for thy good'. George Wilkins, generally accused of being the collaborator in 'Pericles' and by Professor Wilson also supposed to be the collaborator in 'Measure for Measure', wrote a novel on the subject after the production of the play. Sir Edmund Chambers notes that in a few places Wilkins uses scraps of blank verse from the play; but he also notes the curious fact that he uses scraps of blank verse which are *not* in the play, at least as it has come down to us. One of these scraps which Sir Edmund isolates is actually the end of the bawdyhouse scene, and instead of 'if thou dost hear from me it shall be for thy good' it runs 'If you but send to me I am your friend'.[3]

There are alternative renderings of the second scene in 'Measure for Measure', and Professor Wilson may be right in suggesting that the 'reviser' was providing 'fat' for the actor who played Lucio. Parolles is certainly a remarkable bit of writing-up for the same type of actor. I get a very strong impression that the collaborator was a stage director. I can imagine no one else who could possibly have had the last word in collaboration with Shakespeare. The last act of 'The Merry Wives of Windsor', the Witches' scenes in

[1] *Per.*, I. I.   [2] *Per.*, IV. 5.   [3] *William Shakespeare*, I. 526.

'Macbeth' and particularly 'Pericles' look very like the work of somebody who was responsible for spectacular effects. Again, the abrupt opening of 'Measure for Measure' ('Escalus!—My Lord?'), which to Professor Wilson suggests a cut, to me suggests a man murmuring sadly, 'I never can get Will to identify his characters at once.' There are many indications that he was concerned with the reaction of players to long speeches, as in his undramatic 'Yes' and 'No'; 'With child perhaps?' even to the limits of absurdity in:

| Duke. | You will demand of me why I do this? |
| Friar T. | Gladly, my lord.[1] |

Shakespeare's friends in the company after the death of Augustine Philips seem to have been Burbage, Hemings and Condell. If Professor Wilson is right in his view that 'Measure for Measure' was 'revised' in the interests of the actor who played Lucio, Burbage is ruled out. Hemings seems to have been business manager rather than stage director, and certainly if there is anything in the tradition that he played Falstaff, he is ruled out. By a process of elimination we arrive at Henry Condell, a dark horse of whom we know little but that he, like Hemings, set his name to the immortal dedication of the Folio to the Herberts: 'For when we value the places your H.H. sustain, we cannot but know their dignity greater than to descend to the reading of these trifles.' That, one feels, is how the collaborator of 'Measure for Measure' ought to have written.

[1] *M. for M.*, I. 4.

XI

WITH these two plays, 'Macbeth' and 'Pericles', I should feel inclined to agree with Sir Edmund Chambers that Shakespeare suffered a nervous breakdown, and assume that he had been compelled to call in the assistance of a hack, but that they seem to be followed by the perfectly normal 'Antony and Cleopatra' which for me has always been the greatest of the tragedies. I have no doubt that Shakespeare intended it, like 'Coriolanus' and 'Timon of Athens', as satire, because his misanthropy was steadily gaining on him, and the central figure is not so much Antony or Cleopatra as Enobarbus, the mocker. Antony himself is deliberately caricatured in the scene in which he addresses his 'sad captains' with the intention of making them weep—the old charmer of 'Julius Caesar' having a final fling. But in the process Shakespeare fell in love with Cleopatra himself, and by playing upon the antithesis in himself succeeded in transforming her into a universal figure like Shylock or Falstaff; so that while in 'Coriolanus' and 'Timon' the storm of misanthropy blows itself out, Cleopatra stands up to it and when she falls, falls like a tower.

She may be drawn from the same model as Cressida; I am inclined to think that Shakespeare imagined an Egyptian proper—a gipsy. Never was there a less queenly queen: she is as common as dirt; she lies, wheedles, deceives, screams, sulks, bites and makes love with the tireless, unself-conscious abandonment of an old tinker woman, yet never forfeits our sympathy. If she is not played in this way, as a character part, there is no play. She jokes her way to the highest peaks of tragic poetry, and even an all-merciful God will scarcely forgive an actress who omits to smile at the last 'Peace! Peace! Dost thou not see my baby at my breast that sucks the nurse asleep?' Cleopatra is not being acted at all unless the actress hears the magnificent poetry from far away, as though it were being spoken by someone else. Let her try to take advantage of it and illusion vanishes. To herself Cleopatra is simply a poor girl what's had rotten bad luck with her gentleman friends: it is only to the rest of the world that she is 'a lass unparalleled'.

In fact, the only rule for any production of 'Antony and Cleopatra' is to look after the comedy and let the tragedy look after itself—as it will. Whenever the play fails it is because unconsciously the actors are playing against the lines instead of at once throwing themselves heart and soul into the comedy of the opening scenes. There is no other way to get an audience to accept a tragic heroine who bolts from the battlefield with the gadfly on her, 'like a cow in June',[1] and a middle-aged lover who bolts after her 'and leaves his navy gazing'.[2] Even in phrases like these one can hear the harsh, satiric quality of the verse. Though the romantic in Shakespeare glories in it all, the realist, thinking as in 'Troilus and Cressida' and 'Hamlet' of the absurdity of the reasons for war, keeps reiterating those images of 'the three-fold world divided'; balancing the ecstasies and rages of the middle-aged lovers with the cosmic consequences of their behaviour. 'Let Rome in Tiber melt and the wide arch of the ranged empire fall'; 'so half my Egypt were submerged and made a cistern for scaled snakes'; Antony with 'superfluous kings to be his messengers'; Caesar, 'the universal landlord', with his army, 'the world's great snare' and 'a Queen to be his beggar'—never until the last great shriek of 'The crown of the world has fallen' does the roar of mockery cease.

[1] *A. & C.*, III. 9.   [2] *A. & C.*, III. 13.

It was certainly at this time that Shakespeare began to scribble in the prose revisions of the quarrel scene in 'Julius Caesar'. In the original play Brutus and Cassius had quarrelled about Cassius' weakness for graft; Shakespeare, rightly considering the motive too abstract for tragedy, revised with the idea of making Brutus hear first of Portia's death. In his later work he had a great fondness for words repeated dully as though the hearer could not quite grasp their full significance or was too full for speech as in Emilia's inert 'My husband?'[1] But in the Roman plays the repetition is even duller, like a roll of muffled drums. At its humblest (in 'Timon of Athens') it is:

> —Alcibiades is banished; hear you of it?
> —Alcibiades banished![2]

In 'Coriolanus' it is:

> —At Antium lives he?
> —At Antium.[3]

And again:

> —Coriolanus banished!
> —Banished, sir.[4]

In 'Antony and Cleopatra' the echo has been developed until it has a sinister sound which is like distant thunder.

> —Dead then?
> —Dead.[5]

Or—most striking of all:

> —Fulvia is dead.

[1] *Oth.*, v. 2. [2] *Tim.*, iii. 6. [3] *Cor.*, iii. 1. [4] *Cor.*, iv. 3. [5] *A. & C.*, iv. 14.

131

—Sir?
—Fulvia is dead.
—Fulvia?
—Dead.[1]

The revision of the fourth act of 'Julius Caesar' consists mainly of echoes which almost look as though they had merely been scribbled on the margin of the playbook and incorporated by the printer. There is first the false echo of the quarrel scene (I have italicised what I think to be revision).

—You wrong me every way, you wrong me, Brutus,
 I said an elder soldier, not a better.
 Did I say better?[2]

Immediately on top of this comes a long roll of echoes.

—When Caesar lived he durst not thus have moved me.
—Peace, peace, you durst not so have tempted him.
—*I durst not?*
—*No.*
—*What? Durst not tempt him?*
—*For your life you durst not.*

Then the scene draws to a close with an echo of Fulvia's death but more cunningly done.

—*Portia is dead.*
—*Ha? Portia?*
—*She is dead.*
—*How 'scaped I whipping when I crossed you so?*

After one minor repetition (—*And died so? —Even so.*)

[1] A. & C., I. 2.   [2] J.C., IV. 3.

132

the drink goes round. Messala and Titinius arrive and
Shakespeare drops his echo, a mere whisper but a marvel
of dramatic subtlety—*Portia, art thou gone?* But still the
little tune continues to run in his head, and when Brutus
makes his report it breaks out again. Notice how it seems
to revolve about the idea of death, as though Shakespeare
found the wonder of it inexhaustible.

> —Mine speak of seventy senators that died
>   By their proscription, Cicero being one.
> —*Cicero one?*
> —*Cicero is dead.*

For the fanciful, there is plenty of material in Shakespeare's work at this period. In 1609, whoever was responsible, the sonnets were published, and when Coriolanus
says 'Like a dull actor now I have forgot my part' it is as
though he were echoing 'the unperfect actor on the stage
who with his fear is put beside his part', and when Volumnia
cries 'for how can we, alas, how can we for our country
pray?' it is as though the cadence of 'How can it, oh, how
can love's eye be true?' were ringing in Shakespeare's head.
'Coriolanus', thanks to the fact that it is history, can only
half express Shakespeare's loathing for humanity in the
mass, but in 'Timon of Athens' all hell breaks loose. It is
a curious text, more draft than play-book with passages in
Shakespeare's maturer style oddly intermixed with rhymed
verse in the manner of 'Macbeth' and the other doubtful
plays, but however it came to be written it could never
have been successfully produced for everything in it flows
in the same direction. The misanthropy which up to this
we have seen only in particular manifestations as hatred of
the populace, of sex and of society, reveals itself as hatred
of life. Timon eggs on the whores, 'that their activity may
defeat and quell the source of all erection'; Nature is told

to 'ensear her fertile and conceptious womb' that it may 'no more bring out ungrateful man'; man is to be utterly destroyed 'that beasts may have the world in empire'.

There is a similar outburst of misanthropic frenzy in Swift after Stella's death, and at the risk of being fanciful, I cannot help wondering whether the loss of someone who had been dear to him had not left that drum-roll in Shakespeare's mind which he heard and re-heard in the tone of every voice.

  —Fulvia is dead.
  —Sir?
  —Fulvia is dead.
  —Fulvia?
  —Dead.

XII

Aᴼᴛᴇʀ that rattle of muffled drums in 'Julius Caesar', Shakespeare's place is with the poets rather than the dramatists. What the two great masters of the Elizabethan theatre had sought was realism of one sort or the other; Shakespeare a poetic, humorous realism of which the perfection is to be found in the portraits of Shylock and Falstaff, Dogberry and Pompey Bum: Jonson a satiric Renaissance realism such as he achieved in his own gigantic 'constructions' which were the 'Ulysses' of his own day. Baroque drama cut across both tendencies, for it demanded not realism but expressiveness, and Shakespeare, by drawing upon his own fastidiousness and misanthropy, had made himself the supreme master of Baroque tragedy. Only Beaumont had either the poetic or dramatic gift to approach him in that, but whereas the great scene between Melantius and Calianax in 'The Maid's Tragedy' is comparable even with the sleep-walking scene in 'Macbeth', it is naturally Baroque as Shakespeare's is not. Take, for instance, the tapestry scene from the same play, with its ravishing sentimentality, its languorous attitudes, its tremulous repetitions; it is like a piece of Baroque statuary on one of those monuments that John Webster referred to, with real tears carved upon the lovely cheeks.

> Do it by me,
> Do it again by me, the lost Aspasia,
> And you shall find all true but the wild island.
> I stand upon the sea-beach now, suppose,
> Mine arms thus, and mine hair blown with the wind,

Wild as that desert, and let all about me
Tell that I am forsaken.[1]

Beaumont, with his 'take this little prayer' type of sentimentality, is the pure Baroque virtuoso, delighting in the
effectiveness of his own situations, whereas Shakespeare
can write only out of his own heart, by drawing upon his
own experience, and when the storm of misanthropy blows
itself out, as it does in 'Coriolanus' and 'Timon of Athens',
he has exhausted his dramatic capital. Something of the
kind had happened to him before, towards the end of the
sixteenth century, when his realistic mood, driving him
more and more towards observation and away from his
personal emotions, was petering out in a sort of brittle
comedy. Now, after another ten years in which he had
abandoned realism, his own emotions too were failing
him.

The disintegration of the dramatic personality is reflected
in the continuing disintegration of language. In 'Timon
of Athens' and the Baroque comedies, it verges upon in-
coherence: titles and pronouns are swept into the wild rush
to the abyss; we get 'sirs' and 'shes'; the inversion of the
negative—an early trick of his—becomes commoner, and
there are characteristic words like 'pinched', 'choked' (both
early favourites), 'ebbed', 'dungy' and 'earthy'. It is hard
to believe that any audience understood more than a fraction
of the dialogue which races along, well below the level of
conscious thought, so that we can trace it only by its sudden
rises.

The final group of plays is certainly the most difficult
thing in Shakespeare to understand or explain. All have
certain qualities in common. To begin with, they were
written exclusively for an indoor theatre, and with an
instinctive artist like Shakespeare, not controlled, as Jonson

[1] *The Maid's Tragedy*, II. 2.

was, by a theoretical approach to literature, apparently unimportant external details count for a lot. Exactly as Kempe's departure from the theatre had encouraged the anti-realistic vein in him, so the change from the popular open-air theatre with its audience of apprentices and housewives to the darkness and candlelight of the Blackfriars with its audience of courtiers is reflected in the lack of reality, either objective like Falstaff's or subjective like Lear's. The change did not pass unnoticed by the writers, for though he was still popular, his reputation was on the decline as we see from Webster's malicious introduction to 'The Duchess of Malfi', where he is dismissed as a mere hack like Heywood, and Jonson's reference to 'a mouldy tale like *Pericles*' and his request to the audience that 'they who had graced monsters might like men'.

As the creative impulse is withdrawn from the drama we see more clearly the symbolic skeleton behind. It is possible that all literature is in origin sub-conscious and based upon fantasias of dreams with which the conscious, intellectual mind wrestles until it has given them 'a local habitation and a name'; but certainly with poets and instinctive writers, like Shakespeare, Dickens and Ibsen, any decline in creative power at once causes the shadows of the fantasia to take over control and reduce the writer almost to a state of somnambulism. In the later comedies it is not the fantastic nature of the themes which produces the sense of unreality, but the subjective unreality which makes the themes appear so fantastic. After all, there are wilder improbabilities in 'Twelfth Night' or 'The Merchant of Venice' than in 'Cymbeline', but whereas the first have been passed through a realistic filter, the other has been set down with no attempt to find models in nature for Cymbeline, Posthumus, the Queen or Imogen, so that it scarcely rises above the level of day-dreaming. With a sort of dreadful neatness the characters divide themselves not so much into bad and good as into active and passive; the active, Cymbeline, Posthumus, Leontes, Polixenes, Prospero, all stamped with cruelty and hyper-sensibility; the passive—particularly the girls, Imogen, Perdita and Miranda—transfigured by the blinding light of sentimentality which Shakespeare throws on them.

The pattern stands out clearly in 'Cymbeline', the least happy of the last plays. Here Cymbeline, egged on by his fiend-like Queen, banishes Posthumus, a young man secretly married to his daughter Imogen, whom the Queen wishes to marry to her own son, Cloten. Posthumus, as the result of a bet with a Frenchman about Imogen's faithfulness, becomes convinced of her guilt and orders his servant Pisanio to murder her. Pisanio decoys her to Milford Haven and then relents. Cloten follows her and is beheaded by outlaws (really the sons of the king, kidnapped in childhood by Belarius). Imogen, waking to find the headless body beside her, believes it is Posthumus', and, disguised as a boy, takes service with the Roman ambassador. A Roman army comes to Britain, and the outlaws assist in defeating them, while Posthumus is captured and sentenced to death. After a recognition scene during which Cymbeline sentences practically everyone to death, all ends happily.

Except for one amusing and sardonic little scene between Cloten and Imogen, nothing in the play has been visualised, and its unreality is accentuated rather than otherwise by the stream of echoes from the great tragedies. But then occurs one scene of dreadful reality when Posthumus is awaiting death in prison. 'Hanging is the word, sir,' wheezes the Gaoler. 'If you be ready for that you are well cooked,' and suddenly Shakespeare's interest becomes engaged. In a dreadful parody of the Duke's speech in praise of Death 'which makes these odds all even' and Cleopatra's paean to that 'Which shackles accidents and bolts up change, which sleeps and never palates more the dung, the beggar's nurse and Caesar's,' the Gaoler cries, 'But the comfort is you shall be called to no more payments; fear no more tavern bills, which are often the sadness of parting as the procuring of mirth. . . . Of this contradiction you shall now be quit. O the charity of a penny cord!' It is the Panacea once again; the icy music which blows through all the later plays with its burden of 'No more, no more.'

> Fear no more the frown of the great
> Thou art past the tyrant's stroke.

And suddenly we realise that the Gaoler with his macabre jokes is Hamlet, Macbeth, Cleopatra and Claudio, all rolled into one. 'Look you, sir, you know not which way you are going. . . . You must either be directed by some that take upon them to know, or to take upon yourself that which I am sure you do not know, or jump the after enquiry on your own peril and how you shall speed in your journey's end, I think you'll never return to tell one.'[1]

I can rarely avoid a shudder at the realisation that this is Shakespeare, stirred to vitality only by the symbol of the whore and hangman; that the terrible crisis of soul which had produced 'Hamlet', 'Macbeth' and 'Antony and Cleopatra' has spent itself and descended, like the nobleman's clothes to the actor, from Hamlet to the Gaoler. It is a measure of how the storm of misanthropy has blown itself out.

The pattern repeats itself almost exactly in 'A Winter's Tale'. Here, Leontes, the King, suspects his wife with another king, Polixenes, and after attempting to have Polixenes murdered, he orders the trial of his wife, and first the burning and then abandonment of his new-born baby, Perdita. Antigonous, the kindly old courtier who is compelled to expose her is eaten by a bear. The Queen is

[1] *Cym.*, v. 4.

cleared by the intervention of the Oracle of Apollo (about the only thing which ever could convince one of Shakespeare's jealous husbands) and is then given out for dead. Perdita, growing up as the child of a peasant in Polixenes' country, is courted by his son, Florizel, and Polixenes who shares his fellow-monarch's irascibility, neatly repeats the pattern by threatening everyone with execution. The lovers take refuge with the repentant Leontes, but are followed by Polixenes. The supposedly dead queen, made up as a statue, is then restored to her repentant husband, but this time the recognition scene is omitted. The title suggests indifference if not contempt, and the evasion of the recognition scene is flagrant, and emphasised by the weary abandonment of dramatic illusion in passages like 'There's such a deal of wonder broke out within this last hour that ballad-makers cannot be able to express it.' When a dramatist writes like this he is chucking up the sponge. There is a certain liveliness about the part of Autolycus, yet even this does not pass without a touch of morbidity, for he tells us how the old man's son 'shall be flayed alive; then 'nointed over with honey, set on the head of a wasp's nest; then stand till he be three quarters and a dram dead; then recovered again with acqua-vitae or some other hot infusion; then raw, as he is, and in the hottest day prognostication proclaims, shall he be set against a brick wall, the sun looking with a southward eye upon him, where he is to behold him with flies blown to death.'[1] We need not take the clown too seriously, but after all, Antigonous is eaten by a bear!

'A Winter's Tale' is as much better than 'Cymbeline' as 'The Tempest' than 'A Winter's Tale', for as Shakespeare abandoned the attempt at drama, he gave himself more and more to poetry, and 'A Winter's Tale' is already half-way towards 'The Tempest'. Drama is of a younger house.

[1] *W.T.*, IV. 3.

'The Tempest', one of the most beautiful poems in the world, abandons all pretence to drama; inevitably since the hero is a magician, exiled from his kingdom, who causes the shipwreck of the usurping Duke and his son; causes the son to fall in love with his own daughter, Miranda, and marries them in spite of the rather hopeless plots of Antonio and Caliban. The main difference between this and the earlier romances is that the active principle has not merely absolute power in this world but in the next as well; yet even so, Prospero has still something of the hyper-sensibility of the tyrant and behaves in a quite ungentlemanly way with Ariel and Caliban. The great speech in which he forswears his magic is generally accepted as Shakespeare's farewell to the theatre, though, as in the next twelve months he produced no less than three new plays in collaboration with John Fletcher, his farewell must be taken in the spirit of the positively last appearance of other eminent members of his profession.

Personally, I do not think he had any such idea in mind. That in Prospero's magic he saw something of his own is possible, but equally he saw in it a microcosm of the great magic of the universe, and in Prospero a reflection of the Creator who in his despairing creed he saw as one bringing life into the world merely to destroy it. 'A tale told by an idiot, full of sound and fury, signifying nothing'[1] was what it had meant to him in 'Macbeth'; now it was merely 'such stuff as dreams are made on'.[2] The real difference is not of temper but of distance. The voice of Prospero is the voice of Macbeth, but it has disengaged itself from the coil of ambition and sin, and speaks as if from far away.

In all these later plays it is the remoteness which strikes us most forcibly. Of the three plays he wrote in collaboration with Fletcher, 'Cardenio' has been lost. 'Henry VIII' is merely a job of work in which Shakespeare's part is

[1] *Macb.*, V. 5.   [2] *Tem.*, IV. I.

always the more vivid, but it is as any historical play dealing with a period so close had to be, mere spectacle. There was no reason on earth why 'The Two Noble Kinsmen' should have been mere spectacle, and that is all it is.

There are still scholars like Tucker Brooke who refuse to admit Shakespeare's part in this play, but that seems to me the mere negation of critical judgment. Apart from the splendour of the poetry, unequalled in any other Elizabethan writer, the style has all the characteristics of the later Shakespeare. There is a bumper crop of nouns in 'er': 'purger', 'quarter-carrier', 'approacher', 'charmer' (not a girl but a magician), 'offerer', 'abandoner', 'confessor', 'defier', 'rejoicer', 'decider', 'corrector', and one triumphant synonym for the Creator, 'Limiter'; there are abstracts in the plural like 'shames' and 'decays'; verbs formed of nouns like 'chapel' (to take to church), 'skiff', 'bride' (marry), 'ear', 'jaw' and 'mope' used passively, 'I am moped.' As usual there is the inversion of the negative as in 'If he not answered'.

But the play is undoubtedly a failure. The theme of the two friends in love with the same girl is one which the Shakespeare of fifteen years before would have handled with passion and certainty, but in this play he isn't even interested in it. Apart from the masque scene in which the two friends and Emilia invoke Mars, Venus and Diana, which appealed to him merely because it provided a magnificent opportunity for pure poetry, the only situation in the play which roused him to creative passion was the 'Antigone' theme of the three queens to whom Creon refused permission to bury their husbands. He had lost interest in lovers but was fascinated by the picture of the corpses, 'showing the sun their teeth, grinning at the moon', and he who had shuddered at Yorick's skull and was to leave a curse on anyone who touched his own bones could write passionately of the three widows pleading with

Hippolyta and Theseus on their wedding day (sex and death in equal balance).

> He will not suffer us to burn their bones,
> To urn their ashes, nor to take the offence
> Of mortal loathsomeness from the blest eye
> Of holy Phoebus, but infects the winds
> With stench of our slain lords.[1]

But the one mistake we must avoid when considering these last plays is that of imagining that they express 'optimism' as Sir Edmund Chambers (who frankly dislikes them) calls it, or 'reconciliation' as the editors of the New Cambridge Shakespeare are so fond of describing it. The story of the man who, having emerged from the dark pit of 'Lear', turned his eyes towards the sunlit peace of 'The Tempest' (see any critical work on Shakespeare) is a pretty tale invented originally to explain to non-musical people the difference between the Rasumowsky Quartets and the last quartets of Beethoven, and whether or not it explains that, has nothing whatever to do with Shakespeare.

On the contrary, the late comedies carry on the gloomy imagery of 'Lear' and 'Macbeth' and to it they add a still gloomier imagery of their own. Though for Belarius, 'reverence, that angel of the world' still makes distinctions, it has almost ceased to exist elsewhere; 'the odds is gone', 'all mannerly distinguishment left out', and the end of the world is just round the next corner. The terrible image of the broken seed-pod and the destruction of fertility which we find in 'Lear', 'Macbeth' and 'Timon' is repeated in 'A Winter's Tale' with its 'Let Nature crush the sides of the world together and mar the seeds'.[2] Hamlet's meditation on suicide—personal poetry if ever there was such— the cry of 'That the Everlasting had not fixed his canon

[1] _T.N.K._, I. I.   [2] _W.T._, IV. 3.

against self-slaughter!'[1] echoed by Cleopatra with her 'Is it sin to rush into the secret house of death?'[2] is repeated in Imogen's 'Against self-slaughter there is a prohibition so divine that cravens my weak hand'[3] and Posthumus' 'My conscience, thou art fettered more than my shanks and wrists.'[4] It is the temptation of the abyss; the 'darkness my bride' theme of 'Lear', 'Measure for Measure' and 'Antony and Cleopatra'. The 'flies to wanton boys' of Lear is repeated in the invocation to Jove in 'Cymbeline'—that written according to Dowden by an actor (the breed unfortunately is extinct).

> No more, thou Thunder-master, show
> Thy spite on mortal flies.[5]

In all of them there is, apart from the poetry, an appalling note of weariness, of which the most characteristic word is probably 'ebbed', as though Shakespeare felt that the high tide of life had receded from him and left only mud behind. It occurs frequently, and with it words like 'ooze' and 'mud,' 'bottom' and 'dungy' and not always in 'The Tempest' where the vicinity of the sea lends it a fictitious relevance.

> And the ebbed man, ne'er loved till nothing worth
> Comes deared by being lacked. [6]

> Ebbing men indeed
> Most often do so near the bottom run. . . .[7]

> O melancholy,
> Whoever yet could sound thy bottom? find
> The ooze to show what coast thy sluggish crare
> Might earliest harbour in?[8]

[1] *Ham.*, I. 2. [2] *A. & C.*, IV. 15. [3] *Cym.*, III. 4. [4] *Cym.*, V. 4.
[5] *Cym.*, V. 4. [6] *A. & C.*, I. 4. [7] *Tem.*, II. I [8] *Cym.*, IV. 2.

Therefore my son i' th'ooze is bedded and
I'll seek him deeper than e'er plummet sounded
And with him there lie mudded[1].

I wish
Myself were mudded in that oozy bed.[2]

With Prospero's casting of his book 'deeper than did
ever plummet sound' they make me think less of the brisk
voice of the converted pessimist than of the thud of rain
in a gloomy landscape after the storm has gone by. 'I like
to think how Shakespeare pruned his rose and ate his
pippin in his orchard close' sings the greatest of Shakespearean scholars, but whenever I think of him in those
last years at Stratford it is as a man like the Sibyl whom
Rilke compared to an old castle 'high and hollow and
burnt-out'. Emotionally he was dead years before they
took him from New Place to Holy Trinity; a wraith of a
man with inward looking eyes.

What those plays may be said to represent is stoicism;
the stoicism of the old fighter with his back to the wall. It
is as though the last drop of Christian feeling, of faith in a
hereafter, and in the ultimate justification of truth and
mercy, has been squeezed out, and replaced by that shadow
of classical philosophy he had found in Montaigne with its
good-humoured Latin shrug of the shoulders which
Shakespeare, the islandman, half Celt, half Teuton, could
never emulate. It is probably no accident that from
'Othello' onwards he showed a preference for Pagan and
pre-historic themes which permitted him either to fling his
sceptre at the injurious gods or stoic-fashion to endure
their wantonness. It was scarcely merely because the
Blackfriars permitted such spectacular effects that he wrote:

[1] *Tem.*, II. 3.   [2] *Tem.*, V. I.

145

> Laud we the gods,
> And let the crooked smoke climb to their nostrils
> From our blest altars.[1]

And:

> Let the temples
> Burn bright with sacred fires, and the altars
> In hallowed clouds commend their swelling incense
> To those above us.[2]

It may be merely a fancy of mine, but I do feel there is some change in the two plays he wrote in collaboration with Fletcher, though it may be only another step in that growing remoteness from life which in 'The Two Noble Kinsmen' made him choose for his first act the largely irrelevant theme of the unburied bodies. This play seems to reveal almost a fellow-feeling with the gods. They are no longer the wanton boys who kill us for their sport, but respectable huntsmen for whose pleasures any true follower of the chase like Shakespeare must show respect. There is something of the old humour in the way he addresses Venus, linking her with memories of his own larks in the Warwickshire deer-parks.

> O thou that from eleven to ninety reignest
> In mortal bosoms, whose chase is this (?great) world
> And we in herds thy game.[3]

And again:

> The impartial gods who from their mounted heavens
> View us their mortal herd.[4]

[1] *Cym.*, v. 5.　　[2] *T.N.K.*, v. 1.　　[3] *T.N.K.*, v. 1.　　[4] *T.N.K.*, i. 4.

In the character of Palamon with all his innocence and idealism it is as though the ghost of his own youth were rising before him, a Troilus still undisillusioned by Cressida's lightness. Curiously, it seems to be of Troilus that he was thinking, because Troilus' cry of agony when he realises the unfaithfulness of Cressida—'Think, we had mothers!' is Palamon's fiery reply to rakes and cynics.

> I have been harsh
> To large confessors, and have hotly asked them
> If they had mothers? I had one, a woman,
> And women 'twere they wronged.[1]

The bitterness against women too has gone, and the wonderful poetry, clear, calculated and full of muscle, is the nearest he ever reached to true classical quality, as in that unforgettable epitaph on a girl:

> Who made too proud the bed took leave of the moon

Or the First Queen's wild balancing of the marriage night with the corpses on the field of Thebes.

> When her arms
> Able to lock Jove from a synod, shall
> By warranting moonlight corslet thee, O when
> Her twinning cherries shall their sweetness fall
> Upon thy tasteful lips, what wilt thou think
> Of rotten kings or blubbered queens? what care
> For what thou feel'st not, what thou feel'st being able
> To make Mars spurn his drum?[2]

As I say, it may be only fancy, but for me it is as though once more the rock of personality had split; the old hunts-

[1] *T.N.K.*, v. 1. [2] *T.N.K.*, I. 1.

man become the stag at bay, remembering his own youth and all the joys of the chase, forgives the gods even as they strike him. Once more the ghost of Tarquin is with him, and the theme of the faithless friend is mingled with that of the impartial gods, but by now Shakespeare's spirit is so remote that even ingratitude and unfaithfulness are no more than the sport of children playing under his window in the light that fades over the Malvern Hills. The voice we hear is Shakespeare's but it seems to come from an immense distance, until it too fades for ever.

> O you heavenly charmers,
> What things you make of us! For what we lack
> We laugh; for what we have are sorry, still
> Are children in some kind. Let us be thankful
> For that which is. . . .[1]

[1] *T.N.K.*, v. 4.

BIBLIOGRAPHY AND APOLOGY

In the writing of this essay I have been indebted mainly to Sir E. K. Chambers' 'William Shakespeare', and 'Elizabethan Stage' as well as to the textual criticism of Professor J. D. Wilson in the New Cambridge Shakespeare. In a more general and perhaps more personal way I am indebted to Dr. G. B. Harrison's popular works, 'Shakespeare at Work', 'Elizabethan Plays and Players' and 'Elizabethan and Jacobean Journals'.

I have been compelled to test for myself the correctness of certain ascriptions to Shakespeare and the possibility that certain works not ascribed to him may really be his. These are things which no literary critic, however unscholarly by nature, can take at second-hand. It would be the negation of criticism to treat 'Julius Caesar' as a play of Shakespeare's if there were the slightest possibility that it really was by Marlowe, and to ignore 'Edward III' as a play of Marlowe's if, as I am now convinced, it is an early play of Shakespeare's. But the fact that I have been compelled to do this and sometimes to disagree with the authorities, does not mean that I regard myself as in any way an authority, and where I have permitted myself to doubt, it has been in the spirit of a true child of the Church who unreservedly submits himself to the censure of his superiors.

PRINTED IN GREAT BRITAIN BY
EBENEZER BAYLIS AND SON, LTD., THE
TRINITY PRESS, WORCESTER, AND LONDON